CHARITY'S GARDEN

CHARITY'S GARDEN

PRAYING MEDIC

INKITY
PRESS™

©2025 Praying Medic®

All rights reserved.
This book is protected by the copyright
laws of the United States of America.
No portion of this book may be stored electronically,
transmitted, copied, reproduced or reprinted for commercial gain
or profit without prior written permission from Inkity Press™.
Permission requests may be emailed to **admin@inkitypress.com**
or sent to the Inkity Press mailing address below.

Only the use of short quotations or occasional page copying
for personal or group study is allowed without written permission.

Inkity Press LLC, 137 East Elliot Road, #2292, Gilbert, AZ 85299

This book and other Inkity Press titles can be found at:
InkityPress.com and **PrayingMedic.com**

Available at online retail book outlets.

For more information visit our website
at **www.inkitypress.com** or email us at
admin@inkitypress.com or **admin@prayingmedic.com**

ISBN-13: 978-1947968219 (Inkity Press)
Printed in the U.S.A.

NOTE

This book is the prequel to my first novel *The Gates of Shiloh*. The books in this series are intended to stand alone. It is not necessary to read *The Gates of Shiloh* before reading *Charity's Garden*. However, if you have not read that book, you might consider reading it after finishing this one, as it is a continuation of this story.

1

Snowflakes swirled in the wind, washing the world in white as the milk truck careened down the sloping road, its tires sliding along the ice-slick asphalt. With each twist of the steering wheel, the driver fought for control, but the truck finally crossed the centerline.

The elderly man in the oncoming car had only seconds to react—a gasp, a tightening grip on the wheel, a fleeting prayer whispered into a gray sky. Shattering glass and the sound of crumpling metal punctuated the wintry calm. The car gave way; its front end was now a gnarled sculpture of ruin, steam hissing into the sky, and neon coolant forming a puddle on the asphalt.

Inside, the driver was pinned, the steering wheel pressing against his chest, his heartbeat erratic. Beside him, his wife lay motionless, but breathing.

The wail of sirens grew louder as two emergency vehicles approached. The red lights of Charity McBride's ambulance cast an eerie glow on the pristine white landscape. As they neared the scene, Charity's mind raced at the sight of the mangled wreckage. Although she had only a couple of years of experience, the Emergency Medical Technicians of her volunteer crew recognized her leadership skills and made her their crew chief.

Charity leaped from the ambulance before it had fully stopped. She flung open the side compartment of the ambulance and grabbed a plywood backboard and bag with immobilization equipment, then rushed toward the crumpled car. Her partner followed, carrying a trauma bag and oxygen tank. A fire engine pulled to a stop behind the ambulance.

"Sir, ma'am, can you hear me?" Charity called out.

The man's eyes opened, glazed with pain and confusion. "Help… my wife," he gasped, his breath fogging the frigid air.

Charity nodded, her blonde hair whipping in the wind as she turned to her EMT partner. "We need the jaws of life, now!" she shouted.

As firefighters approached with the hydraulic rescue tools, Charity climbed in the back seat and, after securing his neck in a cervical collar, asked the man where he hurt most. "My ribs," he moaned.

"Sir, I'm going to put an oxygen mask on you. Try to take slow, deep breaths," Charity said as she slipped the mask over his face.

The whine of the generator powering the jaws of life filled the air, accompanied by the crunch of metal as the firefighters began their work. Charity focused on the elderly man, monitoring his breathing and pulse as the rescue efforts continued around them.

"What's your name, sir?" she asked.

"George," he wheezed through the oxygen mask. "My wife… Eleanor…"

"We're going to get you both out of here, George," Charity assured him. "Just stay with me." Although Charity and her team were unpaid volunteers, they worked with precision to rescue the trapped victims. Charity noticed George had an open fracture of his left forearm, but she could not immobilize it until he had been freed from the car. His breathing became more labored. His eyes widened with panic, darting frantically between the rescue crew and his wife.

"George," Charity said, "you're doing great. We'll have you out in a minute."

But George's eyes began to flutter as his consciousness slipped away. Charity checked his pulse and found it barely detectable.

"We need to get him out now!" she shouted to the firefighters, her voice carrying over the sound of the generator.

With a final screech of twisting steel, the jaws of life tore away the last of the wreckage. Charity and her team moved swiftly, sliding him onto a backboard.

"He's in cardiac arrest!" Charity called out. "Start CPR!"

As her partner began chest compressions, Charity provided mouth-to-mouth resuscitation. The firefighters who had been treating Eleanor removed her from the wreckage and placed her on a backboard, then immobilized her broken legs. Both patients were loaded into the ambulance.

The siren wailed as the ambulance traversed the snow-covered roads toward the hospital. Inside, Charity squeezed the bag-valve mask, forcing oxygen into George's unresponsive lungs, while her partner performed chest compressions.

"Come on, George," she whispered, sweat beading on her forehead. Beside George, Eleanor lay on the bench seat, still unconscious, with two EMTs treating her injuries.

Suddenly, George's body convulsed. Charity closed her eyes as a stream of vomit erupted from his mouth, splattering across her face. She grabbed a towel and wiped off her face, then she and her partner released the gurney straps and turned the backboard on its side, allowing the vomit to drain from his mouth. She turned on the portable suction machine, cleared the contents from George's mouth, laid the backboard flat, and continued squeezing the bag valve mask. Charity looked at her partner, a short, stocky man in his twenties whose black hair was drenched with sweat. "Jake, do you need a break?"

Jake quietly counted compressions. "Let's switch at the end of my next compression cycle."

A moment later, Jake stopped compressions. Charity felt for a pulse.

"Nothing," she said and crawled behind Jake to continue chest compressions. Jake took over ventilations.

"What's our ETA?" Charity shouted to the driver.

"Five minutes!" came the reply.

"Call the ER," Charity said, "and tell them we have two elderly MVA victims, one in cardiac arrest, the other is unresponsive with multiple extremity fractures."

"Will do," the driver replied.

Charity continued chest compressions. "Come on, George," she said, willing life back into him. "Your wife needs you."

The ambulance came to a halt outside the emergency room doors. In a flurry of motion, the team rushed George's stretcher into the hospital while a second gurney was brought to the back of the ambulance. Eleanor was moved onto it and taken inside.

Charity gave the emergency room physician a report. "Elderly male, cardiac arrest following MVA. He was pinned behind the steering wheel. CPR in progress for approximately fifteen minutes." Charity and Jake transferred George to the ER bed while an ER technician took over chest compressions.

Charity wheeled the gurney outside to the ambulance bay,

where she found a hose and began spraying off blood and stomach contents from the gurney's mattress. Absent-mindedly, her gaze followed a blood clot as it mingled with motor oil and radiator coolant meandering toward a drain as the stream from her hose melted the new fallen snow. She knew George would soon be pronounced dead and wept as the last minutes of his life swept over her. She removed a wad of half-digested celery from her hair and tossed it on the ground. As she stood there, adrenaline ebbing from her body, she felt the tug of something beyond the physical realm.

Charity's shadow, cast by the emergency department bay lights, stretched across the pavement, reaching into the dimmer recesses where unseen eyes watched.

Zolgreth stood nearby, observing her. His demonic form, twisted over the millennia by envy and spite, clung to the darkness. His heart filled with malice as he watched the woman who stood there, representing everything he was not—a being born of light unknowingly engaged in a spiritual battle. Charity was oblivious to the malevolent being who, at that moment, plotted her demise.

Valdor drew near his pupil. His tall, lean frame was draped with contempt, and his sneering face contrasted the kindness etched upon Charity's features. He surveyed the scene with an arrogant tilt of his head, his lip curled as though the very sight of human virtue soured his tongue.

"Look at her," Valdor said. "The heroic Charity McBride loses another one of her beloved patients." Zolgreth said nothing. There was much he wanted to learn from his master.

"Compassion," Valdor continued, his tone dripping with amusement, "is but a crack in the armor—a gateway."

Though Charity stood just yards away, the gulf between her

spirit and the entities that sought her undoing was vast. She remained unaware of the plotting, her mind immersed in the many transports she had done that ended tragically.

Zolgreth whispered to his tutor, "She does not falter. Each tragedy she witnesses, every scream that pierces the night… they should erode her, yet she stands firm." A junior in the ranks of demons, Zolgreth's failures gnawed at him far more than any reprimand he might receive from Valdor. In her unwavering compassion, Charity had become an enigma he was tasked to unravel, and each attempt only tightened the knotted web of his inadequacy.

Valdor watched Zolgreth wrestle with the problem of how to defeat Charity with a condescending chuckle that encircled them like a ring of smoke. "You mistake her resilience for invincibility," Valdor observed. "Her empathy is the fissure through which we shall seep, turning her strength into her demise." The senior demon straightened himself. "To manipulate these foolish creatures is to craft despair with an artisan's touch. One does not bluntly beat upon the soul but rather, one must carve doubt with patience and precision, finding the most vulnerable spot and pressing on it until it fractures. Watch, listen, and learn, Zolgreth. Her vulnerabilities will manifest, and in those moments, we strike." Zolgreth understood that Valdor's instructions carried the force of command—an expectation of obedience that allowed no room for doubt or question and the promise of severe punishment for failure.

2

15 years later

Charity sat in a chair beside the window of the Bayside Coffee Shop, her hands warmed by the porcelain mug containing her mocha. Seagulls soared serenely in the sunlit sky, carried on the breeze that blew across a bay rimmed with madrona, hemlock, and fir trees, while the capitol building towered majestically above them.

A pregnant woman with a toddler in tow walked toward the door with her coffee. She halted when her daughter's attention was drawn to Charity. Holding out her index finger, she exclaimed, "Mommy… she looks just like Goldilocks!"

Charity blushed and beckoned the girl to come near. The toddler stepped closer, her eyes inspecting what appeared to be a fairy tale character come to life. "What's your name, sweetie?" Charity said.

"I'm Molly," the girl replied.

Charity held out her hand, "It's nice to meet you, Molly. My name is Charity."

The girl reached for Charity's hand, "You're not Goldilocks?" she asked.

"You can call me Goldilocks if you'd like," Charity said, with a smile.

"We'd better get home, Molly," the girl's mother said politely. "A pleasure meeting you," she added as they approached the door.

Charity dipped a chocolate biscotti into the mug, let the liquid drain from it, and bit off the soggy end, savoring it like a sea lion with a freshly caught salmon. A man in his thirties glanced at Charity as he waited for his order to be taken. "What will you have?" the woman behind the counter asked.

"Black coffee with a little cream," the man replied, sliding his credit card across the counter. The barista rang up his order, gave him a receipt, prepared his drink, and handed it to him. "Thanks!" he said before walking toward Charity. "Mind if I join you?"

"Uri!" Charity said with a smile. "Have a seat."

Uriel sighed as he pulled out the chair to her right and sat down. He had not shaven in three days and had not slept in two.

"You look rough," Charity said. "Everything okay?"

"Yeah. I'm working with a woman who has a lot of issues. Her name is Eden. Have I told you about her?"

"The name doesn't ring a bell," Charity replied.

"Nice lady… ritual abuse survivor. Lots of alternate personalities… and demons. Little buggers have kept me busy all week," Uri said before sipping his coffee.

"How do you know if someone has multiple personalities?" Charity asked.

"Sometimes, it's obvious. They'll switch out every few minutes, and the changes are noticeable. One minute they're talking about their daughter's school play, the next, they're talking about demons torturing little girls in a dungeon."

Charity shot Uri a surprised look. "It can happen that fast?"

"Sometimes it will take a minute for the alter that came up to orient themselves, but the switch is immediate."

"Are the changes always that stark?" she asked nervously.

"No. Sometimes they're subtle. Dissociation happens on a spectrum, from mild to severe. Someone might dissociate while driving to work and the only symptom will be amnesia. They won't remember how they got to work. Other than that, no one would notice that an alter had come up and assumed control. But the changes are more severe for some people."

"Like with the woman you're helping?" Charity asked.

"Right," Uri said, "she's the most severe case I've seen. She was subjected to ritual abuse for years and has hundreds of alternate personalities. Over the last year, she's made progress, but she still switches alters several times a day and is continually attacked by demons."

"Is there a chance she can become normal again?"

"She'll never be the person she was years ago. But if we can break her programming, she might become a formidable warrior due to her understanding of demonic tactics."

The next question hovered in Charity's mind like a butterfly trapped in a jar. She feared she knew the answer, and half of her didn't want to know. "How common are these… alters?"

Uri smiled. "Everyone has them."

"Are you serious?" she asked nervously.

"Like I said, dissociation happens on a spectrum from mild to severe and it's caused by emotional trauma. Everyone experiences trauma even if they're not aware of its effects. And everyone has alters to one degree or another."

Charity glanced at her phone. "I need to get to work," she said. "I'd like to continue this conversation at a later date."

"You have my number," Uri replied. "Anytime you want to talk, let me know."

"I'll do that," Charity said. She rose from the table, pushed her chair in, and walked toward the door.

3

Charity sat in the station's briefing room, her gaze fixed on the captain as he rattled off the day's assignments. The words washed over her like a litany of ordinariness—road closures, inspections, training opportunities, community outreach, but they failed to hold her interest.

No sooner had the briefing ended than the station alarm went off. "Engine 35, Medic 3, respond to 22 South Elm Street, female, late forties, severe headache."

Charity and her partner Travis got up and walked briskly toward the apparatus bay. The bay door opened, and the ambulance began its journey. Travis informed dispatch they were en route. Minutes later, the ambulance came to a halt outside the address. Travis and Charity gathered their gear and went inside.

Lieutenant Summers greeted them at the door. "Your patient's name is Marlene," he briefed them quickly while they navigated the narrow hallway to the living room where the patient lay. "She started having a headache this morning; it's only gotten worse.

Her blood pressure is through the roof."

Charity knelt beside the woman and began her assessment while Travis interviewed Marlene's husband. A sheen of sweat glistened on Marlene's brow. "You haven't been to an optometrist or had your pupils dilated today, have you?" Charity asked.

"No, why?" Marlene replied.

Charity turned and spoke to Travis. "Get her on O2 and start an IV," she said calmly.

Marlene's breathing became rapid and shallow, her eyes rolling back as her body seized. An EMT placed an oxygen mask over Marlene's face. Travis tied a tourniquet around her arm and found a vein. When the seizure had ceased, he poked a needle into the vein, attached the IV line, and opened the flow. Charity and Travis lifted Marlene to the stretcher, secured the straps, and raised it from the ground, then started toward the ambulance.

Charity monitored Marlene's vital signs and checked to ensure she was breathing adequately. When they were a few minutes out, she phoned her report to the hospital. "This is Medic 3, we're en route with a forty-seven-year-old female who complained of the worst headache of her life. No medical history, no medications, no allergies. She had one tonic-clonic seizure lasting about a minute when we arrived on scene. Vitals are stable, EKG is normal, O2 sat is ninety-six, temp is ninety-seven, she has a blown left pupil. It looks like she has a head bleed. No report of falling or other trauma. Her Glasgow coma score is eight. IV is established. We'll be there in a couple minutes." Charity ended the call, shoved the phone in her pocket, and turned her attention to Marlene.

Minutes later, the ambulance arrived at the hospital bay, and Charity stepped out. She and Travis wheeled Marlene inside.

"Severe headache—possible head bleed," Charity said to

the receiving nurse as they lifted Marlene to a hospital gurney. There was a quick exchange of information, and Marlene was whisked away.

Travis cleaned the gurney and restocked IV supplies while Charity wrote her report. When it was finished, she took the report inside and left it with the receiving nurse. Charity got in the ambulance and notified dispatch they were available.

As they left the hospital, the radio came to life. "Engine 36, Engine 31, Battalion 3, Medic 3, respond to a commercial structure fire, Main and Fifth."

Travis drove the short distance to the address. As they approached, plumes of smoke billowed into the sky. They exited the ambulance, donned their turnout gear, and then looked for the incident commander. The first fire engine had just pulled up. The lieutenant got out and told Charity and Travis to deploy the primary attack line while assigning the backup line to his crew of firefighters.

After crawling on their hands and knees through the smoke-filled building, Charity and Travis located the fire and extinguished it. They turned and retraced their path back toward the exit following their hose line. As they met the crew handling the backup line, Travis shouted, "Fire's out!" He and Charity continued crawling until they were outside in the alley. They dropped the hose and walked toward the engine. Travis got the lieutenant's attention. "Fire's out," he said. "Can we clear?"

"Fine with me. We'll take it from here."

Charity and Travis opened the compartment doors of their ambulance and shed their wet bunker gear. A firefighter handed them each a bottle of Gatorade, which they guzzled before climbing back into the ambulance.

Fifteen minutes later, Charity and Travis entered the day

room of the fire station, where the lingering odor of smoke from their uniforms met the smell of burnt coffee. Charity silently slipped into a recliner in the corner of the darkened room, trying not to disturb the firefighters who sat before a flickering TV playing a video game.

The respite, however, was short-lived. The overhead speaker called out, "Medic 3, Engine 34, respond to 819 East Market Street for a mental health check."

"Yippee," Charity said sarcastically as she walked to the apparatus bay.

The lieutenant from Engine 34 briefed Charity and Travis as they entered the house. "We have a real winner. A young guy… I'd guess twenty-five years old, has barricaded himself in his bedroom."

"Leave me alone!" the man yelled from the bedroom.

Charity surveyed the house, noticing a television face down on the mauve, deep pile, urine-stained carpet. Its back panel was removed, and its circuit board was exposed as if someone had tried to repair it but had given up interest. Random framed pictures collected from Goodwill hung on the walls. Full garbage bags were heaped in piles around the perimeter of the living room. "I think we can get through the crap piled in front of the door," the lieutenant continued, "but we're going to need an elephant tranquilizer to capture him."

Charity held up her left arm and pointed to her flexed bicep. "Let me at him," she said with a smile.

"Okay, champ, he's all yours." The lieutenant turned, and they followed him to the bedroom, where he instructed two firefighters to remove the hinge pins from the door. They did, and placed the door to the side. They moved the furniture and boxes that were piled in front of the opening. "Go away!" the man yelled from beneath a pile of blankets.

"Sir, we're here to help you," Charity said sweetly. "We're not going to hurt you."

"Demons!" he screamed. "Get them away from me!"

Travis and a firefighter brought the gurney into the bedroom, lowered it to the ground, and then released the straps, allowing them to dangle. Travis produced four soft restraints and handed one to each firefighter and the lieutenant. "Okay, when I give you guys the signal," Travis explained, "we each grab an extremity, lift him from the bed, place him on the gurney, and restrain him."

"Works for me," the lieutenant replied.

Travis gave the command, and the crew sprung into action, quickly lifting the man from the bed and slamming him onto the gurney, where they applied restraints. "Let me go! Let me go, you demons!" the man screamed. He tried to free himself but was too weak to escape their grasp.

"You guys get him settled, I'll call the hospital," Charity said. The firefighters helped Travis move the man to the ambulance. Charity pulled her phone from her pocket and dialed the number for the hospital. "Medic 3 is en route with a male patient approximately twenty-five years old who is having a mental health crisis. He's hallucinating, screaming and uncooperative. No apparent injuries. We are unable to obtain vitals as he is extremely combative. ETA is ten minutes." Charity listened to the reply, ended the call, and walked to the ambulance. She sat in the seat at the head of the gurney as two firefighters observed the still-screaming man, looking for signs that he might have escaped the restraints. The transport was uneventful. They helped transfer the man to the ER gurney while Charity gave her report. After charting the call, she and Travis climbed aboard the ambulance and departed the hospital.

The radio broke its silence. "Medic 3, Engine 33, respond to 528 South Alder Street for chest pain."

Charity sighed. Travis keyed the mic. "Medic 3 en route."

They arrived at the residence five minutes after the engine company. The lieutenant gave Charity the report: "We are seeing a fifty-five-year-old male with substernal chest pain radiating to his jaw. Onset three hours ago. He complains of nausea, but no vomiting, and no shortness of breath. He says he was seen early this morning in the ER for the same symptoms. Doc said it was non-cardiac and released him."

Travis went to the kitchen to get information from the man's wife while Charity began her evaluation. She obtained a 12-lead EKG while the firefighters got a set of vital signs. "So, if I understand correctly, you've had the chest pain for three hours. It's the same pain you were seen for in the emergency room earlier today?"

"That's right," the man said.

"And what did they determine?"

"They thought it might be a problem with my stomach. The emergency room doctor wants me to see a gastroenterologist, but I thought I would see my primary care doctor first."

"Were you going to see your doctor today?"

"Yes," he replied.

"Is your wife able to drive you?" Charity asked.

"Yes, if you think it's safe."

"Let me call the hospital and get their permission." Charity dialed the number for the ER. "This is Medic 3. We're evaluating a fifty-five-year-old male with three hours of chest pain radiating to his jaw. Vitals are stable. EKG is normal sinus rhythm with no acute changes. He was seen earlier today in your ER for the same symptoms."

"This is Doctor Benson. Is the patient Jeremy Franklin?"

"Yes," Charity replied.

"Okay. I saw Mr. Franklin early this morning. I did a full cardiac workup and found nothing. He was given a GI cocktail and his symptoms resolved. It did not appear that he was having a cardiac event this morning. What would he like to do?"

"He wants his wife to drive him to his primary care doctor."

"That seems like a good plan," Doctor Benson replied.

"Thank you, Doctor," Charity replied. She ended the call and relayed the information.

Travis entered the room and motioned for Charity to meet him in the dining room. Charity looked at the firefighters. "Can you guys button things up?" She got up and walked toward Travis.

"What are you doing?" Travis asked.

"What do you mean?" she replied.

"You're going to let a guy with classic cardiac chest pain go to his doctor by private vehicle… Have you lost your mind?"

Charity did not appreciate Travis questioning her judgment. Filled with pride, she replied, "Yes, it's classic chest pain, but he had the exact same symptoms this morning. He was seen in the ER by Doctor Benson. They did a full cardiac workup and found nothing. After a GI cocktail, the symptoms resolved. He's not having a heart attack."

"Charity," Travis said, "you know this is a bad idea. He needs an IV, nitro, and a ride to the ER."

"Travis," Charity replied sarcastically, "did you miss the part where I said I talked to the ER doc and he said it's okay for his wife drive him to his private doctor?"

"This is a bonehead move," Travis said. The engine company had put their equipment away, and Charity and Travis walked back to the ambulance in silence.

Thirty minutes later, they sat in a booth at Bayside Coffee

Shop. Charity's thoughts drifted back to the man with chest pain they had left behind. Travis leaned back against the booth, his eyes on the bustling street, trying to ignore the undercurrent of tension. The uncomfortable silence was finally broken. "Medic 3, Engine 31, respond to 116 East Jasmine Lane for CPR in progress."

They climbed back into the ambulance and went en route. As they pulled into the driveway of a medical clinic, the scene unfolded with a surreal clarity—the cry of a woman caught Charity's attention as she watched the staff from the facility perform CPR on a man in the parking lot. The ambulance jerked to a stop. Charity and Travis got out, grabbed their equipment and approached the spot where nurses tried frantically to revive a middle-aged man.

There he lay, the same man Charity had talked to minutes before, now motionless on the ground. The weight of their earlier decision loomed ominously in her mind as she attached defibrillation pads. "Stop CPR," she barked. "Charging to 200." When the defibrillator had charged, she yelled, "Clear!" The man's body jolted with the charge. She checked the monitor screen and felt for a pulse. "Continue CPR." The engine company had arrived and relieved the nurses. A firefighter performed compressions while Charity guided a plastic tube into the man's trachea. She attached a bag valve mask. "Bag," Charity said to an EMT nearby. He obediently squeezed the bag as she assessed his breath sounds. Satisfied, she secured the tube in place. Travis had already started an IV and administered an amp of epinephrine.

"Epi on board," he yelled to the lieutenant, who charted their actions. The resuscitation continued, but the monitor displayed a flat line. Charity knew there was no hope but also knew if the man died, it would lead to severe consequences for her.

"Breathe, damn you!" she whispered as the doomed rescue efforts continued.

"Charity, we've done all we can," Travis said quietly, his hand on her shoulder.

"Call the hospital," Charity said with a tone of resignation. Travis called the hospital and received orders to end the resuscitation, along with an official time of death.

The world contracted, leaving only the grieving wife, whose sobs filled the air—a dirge for her husband whose death was partly Charity's fault. She knew that they would not be in this predicament if she had heeded Travis's warning and transported him when they first saw him at his home.

Charity faced the crying woman. She thought about offering a condolence but burst into tears and walked slowly toward the ambulance. Travis stood before the woman. "Ma'am, I'm so sorry," he whispered. He watched the woman crumple on the sidewalk.

Travis met Charity in the back of the ambulance, where she was cleaning and restocking their equipment between sobs. He said nothing but began organizing their gear to prepare for the next call. The lieutenant from Engine 31 came to the ambulance and addressed Travis.

"I just got off the phone with the captain. When you have everything squared away, put yourself out of service and meet me at the station for a debrief."

"Will do," Travis replied softly.

The fire station felt oppressively still as Charity entered it. She took her seat at the table in the briefing room. Travis took a seat beside her. The other crew members gathered around the table. The captain sat at the head of the table, his gaze somber.

"We need to discuss the events of today," he began. "Charity, you were the primary medic on both calls. Let's start with what you recollect. First, let's review the call for chest pain and then the cardiac arrest."

"I screwed up," Charity blurted out. "Travis warned me, but I didn't listen and now he's dead."

"Firstly," the captain interrupted, his hands clasped, "no one is laying fault at your feet. We have protocols for a reason, and today's outcome… it was tragic."

Charity listened to each word, but they only added to the burden she felt.

"I understand, sir," she said. "But I want you to know I take full responsibility for the decisions I made."

The captain nodded. "This isn't the time for placing blame. Right now, I need an accurate account of what happened. Down the road, there will be an inquiry. There are legal implications to consider," he stated, "but today, I simply need to you tell me what happened on the two calls."

Charity rehashed the events as the captain jotted notes. "When you called the hospital and got permission to release him to his wife's care, I assume the call is recorded somewhere."

"Yes," Charity replied. "All calls to base station are recorded."

"And I assume your paperwork contains a release signed by the patient?" he asked.

"That's correct," she replied. Charity then explained their arrival at the doctor's office, the attempted resuscitation, and the call to the hospital to end the rescue efforts.

"Did you talk to the wife at that time?"

Tears flowed from Charity's eyes, "No."

The captain went around the room, asking each person what they saw and what they said to the wife. When he had gathered the information he needed, he dismissed the crews except Travis and Charity. After the room had cleared, he turned to them. "I'm putting you both on paid leave for the rest of the day. Your replacements are on the way. If you think you might need counseling, check in with human resources before you go home." Travis and Charity thanked him, rose from the table, and left the room.

4

Two weeks later

Charity prepared to step off the ski lift as the chair approached the platform. To her right, three firefighters adjusted their goggles and tightened their gloves in anticipation of the day's first run. It had snowed the night before, and the mountain loomed silent and grand before them, its undisturbed powder a canvas awaiting the arcs of their descent.

Charity clicked into her snowboard, the bindings snapping shut with a satisfying clack. With a nod to her companions, she leaned forward and allowed gravity to pull her slowly downward. Charity led the way, her board cutting a clean line through the untouched powder. She wove between trees that rimmed the run, their branches heavy with winter's touch.

The mountain's vastness made her feel both insignificant and eternal. The thrill of the descent, the bite of the wind—it all culminated in a feeling of being utterly alive. In these moments, Charity wasn't just moving across the earth; her mind melded with the mountain as it murmured secrets only she could hear.

As the slope leveled and the world ceased its rushing blur, Charity coasted to a gentle stop, the laughter and cheers of the firefighters rising like a chorus behind her. They, too, had felt the mountain's call and had answered it. They cruised effortlessly to the line where dozens of others waited patiently for a ride to the top.

Once again, they exited the chair at the top of the mountain and formed a group. "Last one to the bottom buys beer," Tony said. The gauntlet had been thrown. And then, with a nod from Charity, they were off—a blur of color against a white backdrop, carving their paths down the slope. The rush of air filled Charity's ears. Twists and turns became their language, a conversation held not in words but in arcs and bounds upon the snow. Tony was fearless, taming the difficult parts of the hill. But Charity attacked the slope with reckless abandon. As the incline softened, signaling the end of their contest, Charity zipped past Tony and coasted into the clearing just ahead of him.

"Charity's the queen of the mountain," Allan said as they coasted toward the line for the lift.

"Queen today, maybe," she responded. "But every run's a new chance. Next time, I'll give you a head start."

"Not in a million years," Tony replied.

"Who's up for a real challenge?" Charity asked, the words carried on puffs of breath that danced away into the frigid air.

A chorus of affirmatives met her question. At the top of the mountain, they surveyed a run that began with a steep pitch. After a few hundred yards, it wound through dense trees and treacherous drop-offs.

"That's crazy," Allan said.

"I'm out," chimed Tony, pointing his board toward an easier path. "See you guys at the bottom." Her friends turned away one by one and waved to her as if to say farewell.

Charity dropped over the edge and plunged into the run, the world falling away until there was nothing but the rush of wind, and the hiss of snow. She leaned into the descent, her body an extension of her will, carving a path of defiance.

The mountain tested her skill, throwing twists and turns that demanded complete focus and rapid reflexes. She sailed over moguls, her shadow racing beside her like a dark wraith. The air was bitter cold, yet within her burned a fire that no frost could touch—a flame of freedom. Each turn was an amalgam of speed, precision, and strength. The trees blurred past as she zipped through the narrow fairway of white amid the forest. And when the run finally leveled out, she came to a halt near the lift, spraying a fan of snow crystals into the air at those who watched her. The firefighters soon joined her at the bottom, where they boarded the chair for another ride to the top.

Tony looked at Charity respectfully. "How long have you been snowboarding?"

"My dad first brought me here when I was five," she said, fondly recalling the memory. "Nearly broke my leg on the bunny hill," she added, laughing.

Tony looked at her. "That run isn't a hill. It's a cliff. Aren't you afraid of dying?"

"Tony," Charity replied, "we run into burning buildings for a living."

"Touche," Jasper said as they prepared to exit the lift. The chair creaked as it approached the snow-covered platform. The foursome abandoned the chair and descended the gentle slope while discussing which run to take next. To their left was a run they had not yet considered, and they agreed to try it. Their boards carved the snow as they approached a narrow chute at the top of the run. They bunched together as they made their way westward before exiting the snowy canyon, which opened into a broad slope, its midsection peppered with moguls.

Charity allowed her friends to lead, preferring to stand as rear-guard this time. She watched them weave and jump as they descended, keeping as close to them as possible without risking a collision. There was a comfort they offered, more than mere camaraderie. In their midst, she felt safe from whatever evils the world might unleash upon her. Once more, the slope plateaued, and they merged into a cluster of colored nylon clothing at the bottom.

"I don't know about you guys, but I have to pee," Charity confessed. The foursome unclipped from their boards and approached the lodge nestled nearby—a quaint structure of wood and stone that offered rest and refreshment. Inside, the aroma of spiced cider and the fireplace crackle welcomed them.

They settled around a wooden table and began shedding layers of clothing and stretching out sore muscles. Charity disappeared briefly and rejoined them minutes later. They recounted their feats and spills on the slopes, laughter mingling with the steam rising from their mugs.

"Did you see me catch that air? I could swear I was flying," Jasper boasted.

"More like flailing," Tony countered, earning the usual round of chuckles.

Charity watched her friends, their faces animated as they retold their adventures. The din of laughter and clinking mugs warmed her as much as the coffee she sipped.

Thirty minutes had passed when Tony finally asked, "Hey, Charity, ready for another run?"

She smiled and watched her friends pull their winter clothes on, ready to conquer the slopes again.

"Ready when you are," she said, pulling her coat on.

After they had exited the lift, Charity led the charge, her snowboard making graceful moves in the compacted snow. Down they went, carving paths, their laughter mingling with the wind. Tony stayed close to Charity, occasionally cutting in front of her as they approached a sharp turn.

"Slow poke!" he yelled, zooming past her with a spray of snow.

Charity laughed as she watched Jasper execute a less-than-graceful 180-degree rotation coming off a mogul. He landed on the edge of the board and fell face-first, then slid helplessly downhill, coming to rest on the upslope of the next mogul.

Tony coasted to a halt beside Jasper and then looked toward the others. "Watch out for the roadkill!" he shouted. The rest of the group congregated around Jasper, their concern giving way to chuckles when they realized he was uninjured. Jasper, now upright, brushed the snow from his jacket, his cheeks rosy not just from the cold but from embarrassment.

As the sun met the mountaintop, casting long, golden fingers across the snowy expanse, the group gathered again at the top of the slope. This time, there was a collective pause, a silent acknowledgment that this would be their final descent of the day.

"Last run," Charity said, "Let's make it count."

They pushed off together, moving en masse down the mountain. It was too late in the day, and they were too tired to perform acrobatics. This time, they enjoyed each other's company. And when they reached the bottom, their legs aching and their arms stiff, they unclipped from their boards and walked toward the parking lot.

"Today was epic," Tony said to Charity. "Next time, maybe I'll give that cliff a try."

"You only live once," Charity replied. "But if you do it right, once is enough." The banter continued as they packed their gear into their vehicles. "Take care, everyone," she called out as they parted ways. "And drive safe!"

"See you at the station, Charity," they echoed back, waving from car windows and half-closed doors.

Watching her friends pull away, their taillights glowing like fireflies against the night, Charity felt a sense of belonging. And, as she drove down the winding road leading away from the mountain, for the first time today, she thought about her husband Michael, who waited for her at home.

5

Charity opened the door to her house. In the living room, she shrugged off her jacket, the fabric whispering its dissent as it slipped from her shoulders, settling onto the back of a chair. Michael sat at the kitchen table, unmoving and silent. His laptop opened before him; he glanced at Charity, then looked back at his computer screen as she unlaced her boots.

"Where have you been?" he asked, his voice a wind that extinguished her exuberance.

She hesitated. A sigh escaped her lips while her shoulders drooped under the weight of his stare.

"Michael, the stress at work is killing me. I needed some time away from it." She recounted the day, her words tumbling out in a rush, but Michael's expression remained unchanged.

"Charity," Michael said, "you didn't tell me where you were going or who you would be with. We agreed we would not engage in independent behavior. It destroys trust. We're in this together, remember?"

"I'm sorry," she said, approaching him. She touched the back of his hand lightly. "I know we agreed, but I…" Her eyes searched his, looking for understanding. "I just needed some time for myself… time to feel the wind and the snow."

Michael turned toward her. "Do you understand what's at stake?" he asked. "Every minute I'm buried in my work, I'm sacrificing the same things you are, so I can finish my degree… so we can have the future we both want. Our future. Together."

Charity sensed the tenderness she once felt for him ebbing away like a gunshot victim's blood running out the door of the ambulance. She drew in a breath that tasted of sorrow and tried again to make him understand.

"Michael, I hear you," she began, "I know the sacrifices you've made—how much this means to you." She stepped closer, her shadow merging with his in the dim light. "But can't you see? That mountain—when I'm there, carving through the snow, the stress disappears. There's no death to worry about, and for a few hours, I feel alive."

The silence stretched into the approaching darkness. "It's always about what you want, Charity. Your needs, your space, your freedom." He ran his hands through his hair in frustration.

"And what about my dreams, Michael? Am I supposed to bury them?"

"Your dreams are threatening everything we worked for!"

"Perhaps your need to control everyone around you is smothering the life out of us." He stared at her, his eyes filled with pain and disappointment. In them, Charity saw no compassion and no tenderness. She stepped back, her decision forming like a sculpture emerging from a monolith of marble. "Michael," Charity whispered, the word a prayer, a plea. "I cannot be the only one to bend."

She turned away and walked toward the linen closet. Her hands reached for the familiar softness of a blanket and pillow—her quiet resignation ritual. Back in the living room, Charity arranged her makeshift bed. She smoothed the blanket over the back of the couch, tucking it under the cushions with precision. Settling onto the couch, she lay there, quietly contemplating her future.

6

As Charity stood in the bathroom looking at herself in the mirror, she ran her hand across her scalp where a patch of hair had been ripped out during a domestic violence call the previous week. A scab had formed over the wound. "Need to color those roots, sister," she mumbled as she left. She went to the ambulance, where a paramedic named Roger waited for her. "How was your night?" she asked.

"One call… pretty boring," he said. "Charity," he continued, pausing until she met his gaze.

She turned to face him. "Yes?"

"We have a problem."

"What's that?"

"Let's inventory the narcs," he said as he climbed into the ambulance. Charity followed him, ready to complete the daily inventory of narcotics at the beginning of each shift. Roger opened the narcotics safe, retrieved the narcotics pouch, and broke the tamper-resistant seal. He removed a morphine vial and cradled it in his hand like it was a nuclear bomb. "What's wrong with this morphine?" he asked.

Charity picked up the vial and held it up to the light, immediately recognizing that the liquid inside was half what it should have been. "It's not full," she said with concern. She tried to spin the cap—a feature that prevents tampering—but the cap would not spin. "It feels like the cap is glued on." She thought momentarily, then continued, "What about the rest of them?" Charity took all the morphine vials from the nylon pouch, held them to the light, and tested the caps. "This one looks okay," she said, "but those two have been tampered with." Dread crept across her face as she inspected the Ativan syringes. The tamper-proof seals were broken on two syringes, and the fluid levels were off compared to the one that still had the tamper-proof seal intact. "So, three morphine and two Ativan are compromised."

"It seems so," Roger replied.

"You know," Charity confessed, "weeks ago, I thought there was something weird going on with the narcs. But being a new hire and working in a department with such a stellar reputation, I figured everything must be okay."

"Well," Roger said with a sigh," everything is definitely not okay. Reporting this will cause major problems. Someone is going to lose their job."

"We have no choice," Charity said, her voice concerned. "We have to report it."

Charity and Roger stepped from the ambulance and went to the paramedic's office. Roger pulled an incident report form from the file cabinet, sat at the desk, and began documenting the discrepancies. When he had finished, he handed the document to Charity. Her eyes ran back and forth across the page, fact-checking each detail. When she was satisfied the details were correct, she scrawled her name across the bottom of the form and added the date. Roger picked up the form. "I'll give it to the captain," he said and left the office.

7

Zolgreth's shadow danced upon the walls of the fire station's hallway as he paced. He muttered under his breath, fears and doubts spilling from his lips like dark incantations. "Mustn't fail… mustn't disappoint Valdor," he whispered, each word dripping with concern. He was drawn to the glow seeping through the fire chief's office door, yet he was repelled by the thought of what lay beyond it.

Zolgreth halted as a slender shaft of darkness formed at the far end of the hallway. Valdor drew near, every inch of his form radiating an air of superiority. "Zolgreth," Valdor began, his voice as that of an inquisitor, "Tell me, are you prepared to weave despair into the fabric of her spirit? To torment Charity until she crumbles?"

"Y-yes, Master," Zolgreth stammered, forcing the words out as if they were shards of glass lodged in his throat. "I am ready."

"Your readiness is not apparent in your quivering stance, nor in the tremble of your voice," Valdor quipped, stepping closer.

"Remember, it is in trials and testing that humans are most susceptible to our devices. Timing is critical, and Charity's time in the crucible has arrived. Our success depends on you."

His words struck Zolgreth with fear. He could not let Valdor down—not when so much was at stake.

"Charity is in a bind, my friend. We don't know precisely how she will react. She may cower in fear before her accuser. If she does, you must magnify her imagined ruin. If, however, she reacts with indignation and defends herself, you must seize the opportunity and tempt her with pride and self-righteousness. Read her emotions. Measure her words and take her in the direction to which she is inclined."

"Yes, Master," the junior tormentor replied. He knew the truth in Valdor's words: humans are unpredictable and prone to both pride and fear.

"Charity," Valdor continued, "is on the precipice. You, Zolgreth, will be the nudge that shoves her into the abyss." His fingers gestured in the air as if to pluck the strings of fate. "Find her weaknesses and whisper doubts and accusations into them. Make her believe she is being unjustly persecuted."

Zolgreth nodded. "Yes, Master. I will not fail."

"Good," Valdor said, clapping his hands together with a sound like the crackling of fire. "For your sake, you had better not fail."

With a nod, Zolgreth turned toward the door and entered the fire chief's office. The room was stark, its walls barren except for the commendations hanging on them.

Charity sat in a chair facing the Chief. Despite the chill of the room, perspiration rested on her brow. The Chief leaned forward. "Charity, I called you here to discuss the results of our internal investigation regarding the missing narcotics. As you know, the urinalysis tests came back negative for everyone who was tested."

Zolgreth smiled and leaned toward his victim. "Don't let him get away with that, Charity. You know exactly why the urine test was delayed. The guilty parties pulled a few strings to avoid being caught."

Charity interrupted, "Chief, are you surprised that everyone tested negative? The urine test was scheduled for Wednesday but conveniently, two of the paramedics called out sick that day. The test was rescheduled for the following Monday, a full week after the day we filed the report. Of course, the narcotics had cleared everyone's system by then. That was the plan."

The fire chief looked at Charity with contempt. "What are you suggesting?"

"You don't think it's suspicious that two of the suspects called out sick on the day they were supposed to be tested? Any objective person would suspect they manipulated the testing date so they wouldn't be implicated."

"Those suspects, as you call them," he countered, "have been with the department collectively for more than thirty years. If one of them was addicted to narcotics, someone would have noticed by now."

"He's covering for the ones who are trying to frame you," Zolgreth whispered.

Charity looked at the Chief with indignation. "So there are people within the department who are above suspicion?"

The Chief's face turned red. "No one is above suspicion. But certain individuals deserve greater scrutiny. There were no problems with the narcotics until we hired you. And by your own admission, you failed to report discrepancies when you first noticed them. That's not just a violation of department policy. It's grounds for a criminal investigation."

"Sir, I filed the initial report. Why would I draw attention to stolen narcotics if I was the one stealing them?"

"You were not the one who filed the report," the Chief retorted, "Roger was. You signed as a witness, and it wasn't out of a desire for transparency. You did it because you had no choice."

Zolgreth, hidden from sight, marveled at her tenacity. He could sense the tremors of fear beneath her determination, the quiet battle raging within her soul.

"At any rate," the Chief continued, "we've concluded our internal investigation and we do not have enough evidence to say with certainty who the culprit is. We're turning the matter over to the police. In that you are the primary person of interest, you will be asked to submit to a polygraph exam. Pending the outcome of the police investigation, you are being placed on administrative leave without pay, effective immediately."

"What!" Charity exclaimed. "You're suspending me without pay? But I haven't done anything wrong!"

"Whether you are innocent or guilty," the Chief replied, "remains to be seen, but for now, you are the main suspect. A detective from the police department will contact you to arrange a time and date for your polygraph. Is that clear?"

Charity's lips parted, but she held her tongue. She rose from the chair, turned, and left. Zolgreth withdrew to the hallway, his task having been completed. Valdor lingered in the hallway like the shadow of an ancient curse. Pride welled within him as he witnessed Zolgreth's work. His smile faltered momentarily as Charity passed by. "Resist if you must," he said with grudging respect, "but it will only sweeten your eventual defeat."

Zolgreth approached his tutor. "Exquisite work," Valdor said, his voice a silken caress. "Your talent for manipulating these foolish humans is blossoming under my tutelage." It was high praise from the senior demon, yet it carried the weight of expectation—an unspoken demand for even greater feats of sabotage.

8

As she pushed the door open, the familiar aroma of home greeted Charity, though recently, it had become spoiled with the sour scent of suspicion. Michael, seated at the kitchen table, glanced up. In that brief flicker of his gaze, Charity read volumes—skepticism in his brow, doubt in the set of his mouth, mistrust in the glare of his eyes.

"Back from work already?" The words seemed casual, but the tone hinted at interrogation. He did not rise, nor did he smile. Charity stood there on the threshold, half wanting to fall into his arms and half wanting to run as far as she could from him. Months ago, a chasm had opened between them, filled with unspoken concerns and mistrust.

"Michael," she began nervously, "I have to tell you something." Her husband got up from his chair and gave Charity his full attention. "Last week, Roger and I filed a report after we found narcotics missing from the lockbox of the ambulance."

"I remember you mentioning that," Michael said.

"Chief Walters suspects that I stole them. The police are investigating. I have to take a polygraph test and they've put me on administrative leave without pay." Charity tried to hold back tears.

"Administrative leave?" Michael said, "That's serious. And a polygraph? Why does he suspect you?"

"Because I'm the newbie. And according to the chief, there were no problems with the narcotics until I was hired. He refuses to consider anyone else, even the two medics who called out sick the day we were supposed to be urine tested."

"I have to give you credit… you never fail to find a way to blame someone else."

Charity moved closer, her eyes filled with anger. "Michael, you know I'm not a drug addict!"

"I'm not sure I know anything about you," he replied. "Three years ago, I felt like I knew you, but lately, you've changed. Or maybe, I'm finally seeing the real you."

"Michael," she said, "think about it. Why would I draw attention to my own actions if I were guilty? It makes no sense."

"Doesn't it?" Michael replied, his arms folded across his chest.

"Every vial has been accounted for on my shifts. Every dose I've given has been logged and witnessed by someone else. My urine test came back clean. Are you seriously thinking I could be a drug addict and you wouldn't know it?"

"And yet, the narcotics went missing after you were hired," he shot back.

"Someone is setting me up," she replied. "It's illogical to think I'd jeopardize everything. My career, our life together, for what?"

"Desperate people do desperate things," he replied.

"Desperate? If I were desperate, I would be clawing my way out of this nightmare, not fighting to keep what I have."

"Truth," Michael whispered. "Why not start telling the truth for a change?"

"Look at me, Michael. Look at who you know me to be!" Charity implored, stepping closer, her eyes begging him to see the woman he once loved. Charity felt the gulf between them widening with each word, swallowing the love that once bound them. "Is this what we've become?"

Charity stood motionless, the last echoes of her plea fading into silence—a silence that only confirmed her suspicion. When she could no longer stand the silence, Charity moved toward the door. Her hand found the doorknob. Turning it, she did not look back at him, for to do so would be to acknowledge Michael's power over her.

"Charity, don't—" Michael's voice cracked the air, but it was too late.

She stepped outside, leaving behind not just a house but the sanctuary they had built together. Charity stood alone, her silhouette outlined against the waning light. With one last glance at the home that had become a courtroom, she turned away, her heart a compass seeking a new direction in the gathering dusk. She walked the path to where her car waited, pulled the car door open, and settled into the driver's seat.

The car's tires whispered along the asphalt, telling tales of a journey without destination. Streetlights flickered past in rhythmic succession, indifferent to her turmoil. Buildings and trees blurred into watercolor washes through the teary prism of her eyes, the world outside mirroring the disarray within. Charity drove, each turn of the wheel mechanical—an autopilot response from muscle memory rather than intent.

The engine's hum turned to silence as her foot eased off the accelerator, the car coasting to a stop on the shoulder of a quiet country road. She stared ahead, the dashboard's soft glow illuminating her features in the twilight.

Clearing the pain of Michael's words from her mind, she thought about her next move. Returning home was not an option. In the distance, the neon glow of a hotel beckoned. She pulled back onto the road and dove toward it. A moment later, she pulled into the dimly lit parking lot, stepped out of her car, and went inside.

The lobby was quiet, save for the soft hum of a vending machine and the distant tapping of a keyboard behind the front desk. Charity approached the desk. The clerk looked up, his face showing disinterest.

"May I have a room for the night, please?" Charity asked.

"Of course," the clerk replied. She gave him her credit card and driver's license. He entered the information into his computer and handed them back to her. "Will you be needing anything else?"

"Nothing else."

With a keycard in hand, she traversed the narrow hallway to her room. Once inside, she sat on the edge of the bed, the duvet pristine and untouched. The room, though clean and well-appointed, offered no peace. She lay down, her body an outline in the dimness. The ceiling became a canvas for her contemplations, each crack a line in the map of her predicament. What path led forward from this desolate place? Where did one go when trust faltered, and the familiar turned foreign under the scrutiny of accusation?

Zolgreth lingered in the corner of the room. "He doesn't trust you," the demon spoke into the stillness, "and why should he, when you've kept so much hidden from him?"

The insidious suggestion carried a morsel of truth. She had

kept things from Michael. But he had only judged her when she shared her struggles with him.

Zolgreth watched with pleasure as a tremor of regret shook Charity's body. He imagined himself as a conductor orchestrating the symphony of her fears; each note played upon the strings of her insecurities.

"Will he forgive you this time?" The demon's question burrowed deeper. "Or will he abandon you, leaving you to face the world alone?"

Charity withdrew a tissue from the box on the nightstand and dabbed tears from her eyes, the demon's words having magnified her fears.

Emboldened by her silence, Zolgreth intensified his campaign, each whisper eroding her self-assurance. "He suspects you… doubts you… how long before he leaves you?"

As the night deepened, the battle over Charity's soul intensified. Zolgreth continued his assault, determined not to disappoint his master.

9

Charity turned the key in the lock; the weight of the day's chaos clung to her like cigarette smoke. She entered her home, a haven that had become a prison filled with suspicion. The fire station's sirens and cries had long faded, but their echoes haunted the corners of her mind as she closed the door behind her. In the dim light, Michael glared at her. "Where were you last night?" he asked.

"I needed space to think. So, I stayed at a hotel."

"Who is he? One of your adoring paramedic friends?"

Charity recoiled as if she had been struck. "No, I swear it's not like that!" she yelled.

Michael let out a mocking laugh. "A hotel, alone? Another convenient lie."

In the living room, Zolgreth lurked, a smirk etched across his gnarled features. "Yes, convenient indeed," he whispered.

"Please, you have to believe me!" Charity implored. When he didn't answer, she turned and walked toward the door.

"Where do you think you're going?"

She said nothing but kept walking. The door swung open. The night embraced her with its cold indifference. Michael followed behind her.

"Running away? That's what you do best, isn't it?" Charity kept walking.

Michael's foot caught a patch of ice, and he landed face-first on the sidewalk. Charity instinctively turned to help him but was met with a snarl of rejection.

"Get away from me!" he yelled, scrambling to his feet with wounded dignity.

"Your face is bleeding," she said, more a clinical observation than a gesture of help. His fingers fumbled with his phone. Charity watched, her breath forming clouds of disbelief, as he dialed 911. The accusation left his lips like an arrow fired from a bow, "My wife—she attacked me. I need help."

"Michael, what are you doing? Stop lying!" She lunged at him to grab the phone, but he twisted away from her.

In the shadows, Zolgreth squirmed with glee, his form imperceptible. A smile crept across his face; the joy of witnessing the false accusation against Charity sweetened the bitterness of his own existence.

"Officers are on their way," the voice on the other end of the line said. Michael ended the call with a tap. As he locked eyes with Charity, a cruel satisfaction burned in the depths of his gaze—a silent declaration of victory.

Charity turned and walked toward her car. She opened the door and took a seat behind the steering wheel. With quivering fingers, she reached for the keys in her pocket. With a turn of the key, the engine came to life. The chill of the night seeped in through the open window, carrying with it Michael's voice.

"Stop, Charity! Where do you think you're going?"

She hesitated, her foot hovering over the brake. "I don't know, but I can't stay here anymore," she said, mascara running down her cheeks.

"Running away won't change anything!" he retorted.

"I don't know what happened to you but you're not the man I married."

As she reached for the gear shift, a police car rolled to a stop behind her, its red and blue lights flashing. Michael gave Charity a sinister smile as he stepped away from her car, allowing the officer to approach. Charity turned the engine off and got out of the car. The police officer drew near. "What's your name?" the officer asked her.

"Charity McBride," she replied.

"Do you mind telling me what happened here?"

"We had an argument and she punched me," Michael said, pointing to his bleeding nose.

"I never touched you!" Charity shouted. "Officer, we did have an argument, so I left. He followed me outside and slipped on the ice. I did not lay a hand on him."

"Ma'am, I'm going to need you to place your hands on the hood of the car," the officer said.

"What?" Charity yelled. She knew resisting his commands was unwise, so she placed her hands on the hood of the car. The officer's hands patted her down in search of drugs and weapons she knew didn't exist, Charity wondered how the man she had pledged her life to could weave such treacherous lies.

"Ma'am, you have the right to remain silent," the officer began, the litany of Miranda rights falling on ears that strained to find the rhythm of justice in them—but there was none.

Zolgreth lingered nearby. "You'll never escape this," he

croaked. "He's won, and you're going to jail."

The officer placed handcuffs on Charity's wrists and guided her toward the police cruiser. The door of the police car swung open with a creak. The officer steered her toward the open door.

"Watch your head," he advised as he helped her inside. Charity ducked into the back seat. The door closed with a resounding thud—a harbinger of other doors about to close.

10

As Charity entered the police station, confusion swept over her—thoughts tumbling like a deck of cards in a gust of wind. How had she, a woman who had always obeyed the law, come to find herself accused and handcuffed? Fear nagged her like the incessant bark of a neighbor's dog. She tried to console herself with the knowledge that God was her champion and, in the end, all would be well. But here, surrounded by other inmates and the blaring noise of the police station, that belief felt distant and uncertain.

A police officer guided Charity to a chair in front of a desk. The handcuffs were released, and her hands were pressed onto an ink pad, rolled from side to side. Her fingers' whorls were transferred to paper with methodical detachment.

"Left thumb... now right," instructed the officer, his voice devoid of inflection. Each press of her skin to paper felt like an indelible stain on her once unblemished life.

The booking officer led her to an alcove and pointed to a phone that sat on a table beside a clipboard. "You're entitled to make a phone call. You can call anyone you want. I suggest calling an attorney. On the clipboard there's a list of public defenders."

Charity sat at the table and, after scanning the list, picked a name and dialed the number. A man answered. "Hello," Charity said timidly, "I need an attorney."

"What is your name?" the voice replied.

"My name is Charity McBride, and I've been charged with assault... I think."

"What is the name of the arresting agency?" the voice asked.

"Olympia Police Department," she replied.

"Thank you, Charity. At this point, the only thing you need to do is show up at the arraignment. Don't talk to the police. It won't help. One of our attorneys will meet you at the courthouse."

"Thank you," Charity said, and she hung up the phone.

She got up and was led down a corridor until she came to an open door. "Right in here," said a uniformed guard, motioning toward a changing room. The guard handed her an orange jumpsuit and sandals. "Go in there and change. Leave your clothing on the hangers and your valuables in the basket."

Charity went into the room and closed the door. She set the jumpsuit on a chair, removed her clothing, and hung her jeans and shirt on hangers. She emptied her belongings into a wire basket. Finally, she picked up the bright orange suit of shame.

"Very chic," she said sarcastically. She pulled it over herself, closed the zipper, slipped the sandals on, rose from the chair, and opened the door. The guard led her down the hallway until they came to another open door. "In here," he said. She obediently went inside.

As the door clanged shut, a blanket of fear enveloped her. She surveyed the holding cell, which housed more than a dozen other detainees. Fear gripped her. She thought of how she might assert herself as an alpha inmate—someone to be feared rather than picked on. She smiled when she saw a familiar face—a woman she had transported many times in her ambulance. Maria had a penchant for wandering into busy streets and getting hit by cars while drunk. "What's up, Maria?" Charity asked.

A dark-skinned woman in her fifties with silver hair looked at her and then grinned. "Dear God in heaven... is that you, Charity?" she asked.

"Long time, no see, amiga! Charity replied. "What did they bust you for?"

"I borrowed a twelve-pack from a gas station," Maria said.

"How rude!" Charity laughed.

"I was gonna bring it back... honest!" she said as the women broke into laughter.

Charity surveyed the reaction of the other women.

"So, blondie," Maria asked, "what did they pop you for?"

Charity hesitated, calculating what would be the most strategic answer. "I beat the crap out of my husband," she replied.

The women responded with a chorus of gasps. "What did he do, cheat on you?" Maria asked.

"Something like that," Charity said, taking a seat at the concrete table in the center of the holding cell. Having established some street credibility, the fear she felt earlier had vanished.

11

Charity moved with feigned calmness toward the waiting bus, fighting off thoughts of dread. She climbed the steps and then lowered herself into the first available seat. The door closed behind her. As the bus rumbled along to the courthouse, it seemed to her as if the world had become disjointed, a bizarre dimension where once familiar elements appeared surreal. Her past, a barrage of moments both tender and terrible, flickered before her eyes—a relentless montage projecting in her soul the mess that had become her life.

The county courthouse loomed like a gigantic guardian as the bus carrying the orange-clad inmates pulled into its shadow. The vehicle came to a halt. With a chime of chains that conveyed captivity and consequence, the detainees disembarked. Inside the building, the air was sterile and cool, untouched by the sun's mercy. They were led to a large office beside the courtroom. Charity took a seat on a hard wooden bench.

Silence filled the space, punctuated by the occasional cough or the rustle of paper as officials passed through. Each sound was a reminder of the system at work—of wheels perpetually turning in a machine that knew nothing of the hearts it judged.

"Charity McBride," said a voice from nowhere. She rose nervously and saw a man beckon her toward a table, where she took a seat in a chair opposite him.

"I understand you're being charged with fourth degree assault," the attorney began.

"I didn't do it," she said, "I intend to plead not guilty."

"Understood," the attorney replied. "The court will set a date for trial."

"Is there anything I need to know… anything I should say to the judge?" Charity asked.

"You don't need to say anything. I'll enter your plea," he replied. "In the coming weeks, if you'd like, you can make an appointment to discuss the details of your case."

"Thank you," Charity said.

The attorney closed a manilla folder and turned his attention to other matters.

Charity reclaimed her seat on the bench. The names of defendants were called. Each time, someone rose, went into the courtroom, and reappeared a few minutes later.

"Charity McBride," the bailiff's voice resonated through the chamber. She rose and walked into the courtroom. The attorney followed her and they both took a seat.

"Ms. McBride, you have been charged with fourth-degree assault," the Judge said, "How do you plead?"

The attorney addressed the Judge, "Not guilty."

The gavel's echo had barely faded when she was ushered out of the courtroom. She returned to the bus and sat beside a window, resting her forehead against the cool glass, feeling the engine's vibrations beneath her. The world outside blurred into streaks of gray and blue. As the bus wound its way back to the city jail, a solemn hush fell over the inmates. Glances were exchanged, each pair of eyes telling a story of defeat or acceptance.

The bus rumbled through the gates of the police station and shuddered to a halt. Next door, the fire station stood like a tombstone mocking her former life—echoing alarms and taunting her with the camaraderie she once had with coworkers who respected her but now viewed her as a criminal.

12

Charity sat in the back seat of the police cruiser as it navigated the streets that led to her home. After a final turn, the vehicle rolled to a stop in front of her house. The officer got out and opened the door. Charity exited the car. "I need to explain a few things," the officer said as professionally as he could. "Your husband has obtained a no-contact order against you." Charity suppressed a gasp, covering her mouth with her hand. "You are not allowed to contact him at any time for any reason, except through an attorney or law enforcement agency. Do you understand?"

"Yes," Charity replied somberly.

"Since a no-contact order in effect, you will not be able to live here any longer. You must make arrangements to stay somewhere else, at least until the no-contact order is lifted."

"What?" Charity said. "Michael doesn't have a job. I pay the rent. It doesn't seem fair that now I have to find somewhere else to stay."

"Mrs. McBride, I'm under court orders. If you don't like the arrangement, you can take it before a judge."

"Fine," she replied with a tone of resignation.

"Your husband is not home right now. You will be allowed fifteen minutes to retrieve the things you need. Put them in your car. When you are done, you must leave. Do you understand?" he asked.

"Wait… I only have fifteen minutes to get everything I need? That's not fair!"

"I don't make the rules, Mrs. McBride," the officer replied. "You have fifteen minutes."

As she walked toward the front door, her mind raced. Where would she stay? When might she return? What should she take with her? Why did Michael get a no-contact order?

Charity shifted into survival mode. She reasoned that she needed supplies to get her by for a week or so, until a long term solution was found. As she stepped into the entryway, her gaze swept over the rooms that once pulsed with the life she had nurtured. The walls, stripped of laughter, stood cold and indifferent. Each shadowed corner whispered of a past that lingered just out of reach, haunting her with echoes of joy now tainted by sorrow.

She approached the bedroom, hesitated for a moment, and then rushed to her closet, where she stuffed items of clothing into a suitcase. With determination, she went to the pantry.

"Food, water, fire, and shelter," she said, rehearsing the preparedness mantra she had taught others. She grabbed cans of food and water bottles, put them in bags, and then carried them outside to her car. She opened the trunk and carefully placed the bags inside. She sprinted back to the front door and back into the kitchen, where she grabbed a can opener, paper plates, plastic forks, and spoons and put them in a bag.

She moved quickly to the garage, where she found her tent, backpack, tarp, and sleeping bag. She grabbed the sleeping bag, took the load to her car, and returned for the rest. She went to the bathroom, where she swiped her toiletries—a tube of toothpaste still half full, a deodorant stick, toilet paper, and an old brush with strands of blonde hair entwined in its bristles. She continued filling bags with items of necessity and depositing them in her car.

The police officer observed her. Charity could feel his gaze, respectful yet unwavering.

"Ms. McBride," the officer finally said, his voice carrying the tone of somber duty, "it's time. We need to be going."

She turned toward him, her lips opening as if to plead for more time, more grace, more anything. But the sight of his eyes—pools of professional purpose—stilled her speech. She conceded to his demand with a bow of her head.

Charity slid into the driver's seat of her car. The tent, backpack, tarp, and sleeping bag occupied the passenger seat. She started the engine and backed slowly out of the driveway.

13

The doors of the bank swept open with a hush. Charity entered the lobby and approached the teller's desk. "Good afternoon," the man behind the teller's window said. "How can I help you?"

"I'd like to withdraw three thousand dollars from my checking account, please," Charity said, handing the man her driver's license and bank card.

The teller entered her account number and name, and a look of confusion appeared on his face. He turned to Charity. "Mrs. McBride, there seems to be an issue," he said. "Here is your account balance." He wrote the amount on a slip of paper and passed it to her.

Charity stood paralyzed. A low fire of aggravation kindled inside her as she realized Michael had drained their joint bank account. She tried to maintain her composure. "May I withdraw one hundred and fifty dollars, please?" The teller nodded and clacked away at the keyboard. Charity watched him count out the bills with a rustle that seemed loud in the hush of the bank.

"Here you are," he said, extending the cash and her cards across the counter with the practiced smile.

"Thank you," Charity replied, her hand closing over the money. The receipt sat beside the bills, a thin white strip listing her balance in stark black digits—a numerical echo of the desolation that had visited her.

Charity departed the bank, her steps reverberating upon the marble flooring. The doors closed behind her with finality, sealing off the sterile sanctuary of ordered numbers and cold transactions. She emerged into the cool air, the sun hanging low in the sky—its light no longer a gentle touch but rather an interrogation of her plight.

She lowered herself into the driver's seat of her car and sat still, her eyes slowly scanning a world that had become alien to her.

"Where to now?" she whispered. The question was not one of direction but of purpose—of meaning amid the specter of uncertainty. The answer lay obscured by the looming shadows cast by her empty bank account and the quickly setting sun.

14

Charity sat motionless. Through the windshield, the sky smeared streaks of crimson across the horizon, mocking her with its vastness and the promise of a night full of questions without answers. She counted the money to be certain she was not hallucinating.

"One hundred and fifty dollars," she whispered, the number a declaration of despair. The currency felt foreign in her hands, once symbols of security, now emblems of loss.

She should have reached out, perhaps to an old friend or relative. But pride barred the way. Whispers of weakness and shame were more than she could bear. How could she, who had bandaged the wounds of others and breathed life into the dead, admit to needing rescue? No, her path lay elsewhere, unmarked by the footprints of others. She closed her wallet with a snap—the sound signaling finality—like the closing of an iron gate.

A thought entered her mind. Near the edge of town, there was a plot of land that, in the summer, was covered with wildflowers.

She had always thought the parcel should be made into a park. She didn't know why, but when she visited the field, it brought peace. She pulled her car onto the highway. A sigh escaped her as she drove toward the city limits, gazing at the darkening road ahead.

"It's temporary," she assured herself, "until I find a better place to stay."

The decision settled in her mind like sediment in a drain after a storm. It was a plan—to be sure, one born of desperation—but it was *her* plan. And in ownership, there was a sliver of empowerment, a shard of light cast against the encroaching darkness.

Finally, as the car rolled to a stop at the edge of the field, Charity killed the engine. The world fell silent but for the sound of her own breathing—steadier now, as if arriving had imparted a measure of peace.

She stepped out into the twilight, the door shutting behind her with a soft click that seemed to echo across the expanse of open land, a place both inviting and intimidating. Charity took it all in—the serenity, the isolation, the wonder, and the possibility of peril. Relief washed over her as she realized that here, there were no prying eyes to dissect her every move, no whispers probing her motives. But trepidation lingered. For all the tranquility the field might provide, it also offered loneliness and isolation. She was not deceived; she knew she faced the daunting task of rebuilding her life from nothing without the help of others.

The air grew cooler as darkness settled over the land. Charity opened the passenger side door and removed the tent, the tarp, the backpack, and a well-worn sleeping bag and set them on the ground. She retrieved a headlamp from the backpack, donned it, and clicked through the brightness settings.

Turning her attention to the ground, she removed rocks and

twigs from the place where she would place the tent. She then spread out the plastic tarp. The tent unfurled with a sweeping gesture that felt almost reverent. She threaded poles through sleeves, their aluminum segments clicking together with satisfying assurance. Her hands worked quickly, assembling the tent. Finally, she fitted the rainfly over it and secured it with stakes.

She unzipped the tent, and the fabric parted, revealing the sparse interior of her refuge. She carried the backpack inside and placed it near the entrance. The sleeping bag rolled out with a soft swish, its downy insides promising meager comfort against the hard ground.

As she nestled the sleeping bag into the corner of the tent, Charity's fingers rubbed the nylon floor, the sensation starkly alien after years of sleeping on a mattress. Here, in a fragile cocoon of polyester and aluminum, she would lay her head beneath the canopy of an indifferent sky.

She kicked off her shoes. Settling into the sleeping bag, she drew her knees close, seeking solace in the warmth of her own body. Outside, the wind stirred, sending ripples along the tent walls. The chill of the night air seeped through every layer of clothing she wore. But it was more than merely the dropping temperature that caused her discomfort. Fear and uncertainty taunted her.

A shadow crept near the tent, the darkness coalescing into a form invisible to the natural eye. Zolgreth lingered at the periphery of her camp.

"Alone, are we?" the demon asked, his voice penetrating the tent. "So certain of your strength, yet here you cower beneath a sheet of plastic. How pitiable."

Charity pulled the sleeping bag tighter. As the night wore on, her fears intensified, spurred by the threats uttered by Zolgreth.

Yet within her, a flame of hope flickered defiantly.

"Your flame flickers," Zolgreth acknowledged, "but the darkness is vast and it will swallow your light whole."

15

Charity emerged from her tent on a frigid morning, the sky awash with pale light. Her eyes scanned the landscape before her. She moved tentatively away from the tent like a fawn walking onto a frozen pond.

Charity's breath formed clouds as she moved deeper into the garden. The once lush foliage now stood subdued by winter's grip. She paused at the perimeter where disorderly patches of flowers made their last stand against the frost, their petals bowing under the weight of ice crystals. Her heart twinged with a pang of kinship; she also felt wilted and weak like them. Charity watched her steps, mindful yet mesmerized by the delicate fractals beneath her feet, a latticework of artistry both beautiful and sorrowful.

A few minutes into her wintry walk, a figure caught Charity's eye, an anomaly in the muted landscape. In the center of the meadow, an elderly man bent over a patch of stubborn greenery that refused to yield to the cold. White hair flowed from beneath a weathered hat, cascading over his shoulders. His hands moved methodically to clear away frost from the partly frozen leaves. Charity stood transfixed, her mind filled with curiosity.

"Good morning," the man finally called out to her without a hint of surprise at her presence, his smile broad and genuine, radiating warmth. He straightened up, brushing dirt from his hands onto his overalls.

"Morning," Charity returned. She drew nearer. "It looks like the cold has destroyed your flowers."

"Ah, but the cold is temporary," he replied. "Nature has its seasons, each with its own purpose. The garden sleeps, but it dreams of spring."

"Is it always this quiet?" she asked, her curiosity piqued by the stillness.

"Every morning is a whispered invitation," he said, "to listen, to observe… the garden speaks in sighs and rustling leaves. It's never truly quiet if you know how to hear it."

A silence fell between them, but she sensed no discomfort. There was no rush, no hurry. The gardener seemed content to work as much as he enjoyed conversation. She tucked a rogue strand of blonde hair behind her ear, the gesture almost lost in the quiet exchange.

"I've always found comfort in the greenery of this place," she confessed. "Even now, with everything so… traumatized, there's something about it that's restful. Almost healing."

The gardener paused, his hands cradling a mound of earth as if it were the most precious thing in the world. "The land listens, my dear. It holds your joys and sorrows just the same."

She looked at him, this man who seemed as much a part of the landscape as the gnarled oak trees lining the property. There was no judgment in his eyes, only the serenity of a still pond. "Thank you," she said.

I didn't get your name," the man said respectfully.

"Charity."

"A beautiful name." The gardener pointed to a cluster of blooms, their petals a defiant burst of color against the frosty canvas. "These flowers," he said, his voice a gentle rumble, "they hold fast through the chill, persevering when all seems lost. Much like the human spirit, wouldn't you say?"

His words were simple yet profound. Charity felt them buttress the walls of her heart. There was no accusation in his tone, no attempt to pry open the doors she had closed—only the sympathetic voice of understanding. "Sometimes," the gardener continued, "it is in the harshest soil that the strongest flowers grow."

Her response was a silent nod, acknowledging that strength often roots itself in adversity.

"Every plant here has battled for its place under the sun," the gardener continued, "just like every person has their own trials to weather."

The gardener recounted the history of a particular rosebush that had been trampled yet still clung to life, blooming year after year with defiance. As he spoke, he tended the leaves and coaxed the frozen stems with a lover's touch.

Gradually, the sun ascended, its rays piercing the thin veil of morning mist. Charity tilted her face toward the sky, feeling the gentle kiss of warmth upon her cheeks. She rose to her feet, brushing off the remnants of frost from her knees. "Thank you," she said, "for sharing this place... these stories."

"Always a pleasure," he replied, his smile crinkling the corners of his eyes. "You are welcome here anytime."

Charity offered a final nod of gratitude before retreating to the garden's periphery. She reached the entrance of the tent, the flap yielding to her touch. She kicked off her shoes and settled into the sleeping bag, seeking warmth while contemplating the morning's revelations.

16

Zolgreth slunk toward a homeless encampment near the center of town, not wanting to be late for his appointment. Nearing a row of tents, tarps, and campfires, he sensed the approach of his master. Valdor emerged from the shadows, the dim light revealing his angular features.

"Zolgreth," Valdor greeted, his voice a velvet caress coated with contempt.

"Master," Zolgreth responded. He could feel Valdor's gaze upon him, weighing, measuring, and finding him wanting. But within that gaze, there was also the promise of dark wisdom—the allure of secrets that could shatter the most resilient of spirits. And it was this promise that kept Zolgreth rooted to his spot, hungering for the knowledge that would allow him to finally break Charity.

"Tell me, Zolgreth," he began, "what progress have you made with Miss McBride?"

"She is alone, sir," the demon began, "homeless and despondent.

It won't be long before I have her entertaining thoughts of suicide."

"And what of the gardener, Zolgreth? Do you think I am unaware of his influence?"

"The gardener... he has Charity's ear," Zolgreth confessed. "I must find a way to destroy her trust in him."

"Ah," Valdor replied, "You have correctly assessed the battlefield. The gardener's influence is critical—we must dispel it immediately."

Valdor spoke with the bravado of a seasoned orator, each word chosen for its ability to intimidate and inspire fear. "Charity McBride is pivotal, a vessel of their so-called hope. Her connection to the gardener imperils our purpose. Should she remain under his influence, others will surely follow. And that, my apprentice, simply cannot happen."

Zolgreth fixated upon Valdor's every syllable, a desperate student before an unforgiving mentor. The shadows of the encampment seemed to lean in, eager for the lesson they were about to receive.

"Failure," Valdor continued, his tone swelling with fervor, "is a luxury we cannot afford! You must strike with precision, my friend, and sever her friendship with the gardener."

Zolgreth's shadow mingled with the gloom at the fringe of the homeless encampment, a dark stain upon the earth that mirrored the turmoil within his twisted soul. He felt Valdor's penetrating gaze upon him as if the weight of his mentor's scorn was a physical thing pressing down upon his hunched shoulders. "Indeed, Master," Zolgreth muttered. His head bobbed in agreement, though internally, he waged a war between his desire to lash out in defiance and the fear of failing in his mission.

Valdor extended an arm. The flickering light from the streetlamp cast long, sinister shadows across his gaunt face.

"Behold," Valdor said, pointing at the encampment, "this desolation is our foundation, Zolgreth. Here, hope is but a dying ember awaiting the crush of our fingers."

He gestured at an elderly man huddled beneath a patchwork quilt of discarded clothes. "See how time has gnawed at his spirit, leaving naught but hollow resignation. He once dreamed of better days, but now he no longer dreams at all."

Zolgreth watched as the man shifted, his movements slow and deliberate, a surrender to the relentless passage of time. "Charity must taste this same despair," Valdor continued, "She must see her efforts as futile, her kindness as vanity—a waste of time. You, my friend must convince her that she has no future."

A woman nearby coughed. Her hands trembled as she reached for a glass bottle. Valdor pointed her out. "Her every cough is a note in the song of hopelessness," he declared. "Let Charity hear this music; let it seep into her soul until her very essence drowns in it."

Zolgreth nodded. Each face told a story not so different from the next—tales of loss and abandonment.

"Remember, Zolgreth," Valdor said as he prepared to fade back into the shadows, "the strength of the human spirit is but an illusion. Break it, and you break her."

The senior demon's form then vanished, leaving Zolgreth alone amid the ghostly figures of the encampment, contemplating the task ahead.

17

During the five days she had been homeless, Charity split her time between the garden and the coffee shop. Her fingers tapped a rhythm on the worn wooden table, the clink of her wedding band punctuating the silence left by a finished conversation. The café hummed with the low murmur of other patrons, but the empty mug in front of her caught her gaze—a reminder of time slipping away.

"I have to go," she said, the urgency in her voice mirroring the glance she shot at her watch.

"Where to? Uriel asked.

"I have a date with a gardener," she replied.

"Is that so?"

"He's a most unusual man," she said. "You should meet him."

Charity rose from her chair and walked toward the door. Uriel followed her, and they stepped outside. "Let me walk you to your car," Uriel offered.

"Thank you," Charity said. They walked through the crowd

and approached an intersection. Charity was drawn to a scene unfolding at the nearby bus stop. A man with a knife in his hand waved it at a group of commuters. Reflexively, Charity stepped toward the man. Her voice was clear and authoritative, "Put the knife down," she commanded.

Uriel watched silently as the man swayed, occasionally swinging the blade toward a bystander.

Charity did not flinch as he waved the knife in her direction.

"Drop the knife," Charity repeated.

Sunlight glinted on the blade as the man, his judgment clouded by alcohol, hurled himself toward Charity. She said nothing but sidestepped the attack. Her fist, however, was not silent—it connected with his nose, unleashing a thunderous crack. The man's body crumpled to the ground like a puppet whose strings had been cut.

"Gary!" Charity's voice cracked like a whip as she leaped on him and began pummeling him with her fists. Uriel watched in horror.

"Who's the tough guy now, Gary?!" Charity bellowed.

The man cursed her through bloodied lips.

Uriel's hand shot out, gripping Charity's wrist firmly. "Charity, stop!" he urged. But she was no longer present; her eyes blazed with a fire that did not see him. "Stay out of this, Tim, she replied. "This isn't your battle!"

"Gary, why don't you show us how strong you are?" Charity said, her fists moving against Uriel's restraint.

"Charity, please," Uriel said again, his tone now a gentle command. "Let it go. You proved your point." Uriel watched as recognition flickered in Charity's eyes—an awareness that pulled her back from the precipice. She released the man, her breathing uneven as shards of broken memories swirled around her.

"Come on," Uri said softly, guiding her from the ground. They moved away from the scene. As they crossed the street, the sounds of the commotion faded into the noise of city life.

"Where did you park?" Uri asked, his gentle but insistent tone beckoning her back from the fog-laden sea of confusion.

She blinked slowly, her gaze drifting across the row of vehicles basking in the late afternoon sun. A flicker of memory ignited within; she pointed with an unsteady hand to a solitary sedan. "Over there," she said. Together, they navigated the short distance to her car.

As they reached her vehicle, Charity's eyes were drawn to her hands, which looked as though they belonged to another—swollen and marred with blood. She stared at them as a silent question formed in her heart: how had they come to be this way?

"Charity?" Uri prodded softly, standing by her side.

She turned to him. "I don't… I can't remember," she said, her voice barely a whisper.

"Let's get you inside. Where are your keys?"

Charity fished them from her pocket and handed them over. Uri unlocked the doors, opened the passenger door, and helped her into the seat. He seated himself behind the steering wheel.

"Charity," Uri began, his voice calm, "can you tell me what happened after we left the cafe? What do you remember?"

She closed her eyes, trying to summon the memories that seemed to loiter just out of reach. The scent of coffee lingered in her mind. "I remember… we were walking," she said, her brow furrowing as she wrestled with the elusive shadows. "And then—we left, and we got in the car."

Uri nodded. "Do you remember the bus stop? "

"No," she said, shaking her head.

"There was a man causing trouble," Uri said, "He had a knife and you… you stopped him."

"Did I hurt him?" she asked, hoping that her hands were not stained with more than just her own blood.

"You beat him up pretty badly," Uriel replied.

Charity stared at her hands. "I did?" she asked, her voice tinged with disbelief.

"You did," Uri affirmed. "But there was more. You called him Gary and you called me Tim. Who are Gary and Tim?"

A single tear traced its way down her cheek. Gary and Tim—the names tumbled from her lips with a shuddering breath as though saying them aloud could somehow anchor her to reality.

"Gary and Tim are my brothers," she confessed. "But why? Why would I…?" Her voice trailed off, choked by the rising tide of confusion and fear.

"Sometimes, when the soul has been wounded by trauma, it finds ways to protect itself," he said, "In moments of crisis, a wounded part of your soul can resurface, and take control of your body in an attempt to fend off a threat. The part of your soul is locked in time and sees the world through the eyes of the girl you once were. The part identifies people—especially threatening ones—as the person who caused the trauma."

"My brother Gary used to beat the crap out of me." Charity said soberly.

"That makes sense," Uri replied. "What about Tim?"

"My little brother," she replied. "He got the same treatment from Gary."

"Those fragments of your younger self are tormented, but they can be healed. More than anything, they need love."

The notion of caring for splintered pieces of her identity sparked a maternal instinct Charity had not known resided within her. In the distance, a church bell tolled, its chimes confirming there was reason for hope. Charity's eyes wandered to the window; the evening light caressed her face, warm and inviting, urging her to embrace the possibility of change.

18

The first rays of dawn crept through the tent, illuminating Charity's face. She lay still for a moment, allowing the warmth to seep into her skin and chase away the remnants of the night's dampness—her breath mingling with the crisp air that had settled in the heart of the garden.

Finally, she rose and opened the top flap of the backpack that guarded the entrance to the tent. She withdrew a bag of dehydrated eggs from a plastic bag containing an assortment of freeze-dried food packages. Next, she located the instant coffee packets and palmed one. She closed the flap on the backpack, then ducked as she exited the tent, her feet greeting the cool, damp ground. She set the items beside the tent and then walked to her car. She popped the trunk lid and retrieved two bottles of water, a camp stove, and cooking utensils, then closed the trunk lid and eyed a spot away from the tent to prepare her coffee and eggs. She quickly heated the water for the coffee, which she sipped as she rehydrated the eggs and warmed them in a skillet over the stove. A few minutes later, only the coffee remained. In the distance, she saw the gardener approaching.

His white hair flowed down to his shoulders. His eyes found Charity's gaze. "Good morning," he said warmly, "The day is young, and the garden beckons. Will you join me in tending to its needs?"

Doubt arose in Charity's mind. "Thank you," she replied, "but I'm not sure I possess the skill for such work."

"Ah, but skill is born from the courage to begin," the gardener countered, "and the soul, much like these plants, requires nurture to flourish. Every gardener lacks skill at first but finds their touch with time." He laid a trowel on the ground before her.

Charity smiled but did not reply. She picked up the coffee cup, water bottles, camp stove, and cooking utensils and carried them to her car, where she stowed them in the trunk. She returned to where the old man stood waiting, and looked at him nervously. Finally, she reached down and picked up the trowel. Her grip on the wooden handle was clumsy, as though the tool were a foreign object. She sighed. "I'm ready for my first lesson."

The old man turned and walked into the garden for several hundred feet, with Charity following. He stopped and pointed to a young sapling bending beneath the weight of an unseen burden. He mounded the soil around the base to give it strength. Charity helped him. Her fingers, guided by his tender instruction, moved through the soil, finding purpose in the simple act of gardening.

"Even the strongest tree once stood small against an imposing environment. But with care and time, it stretches toward the heavens, unafraid of the distance it must travel. You too shall find your way out of the shadows of others and into the light."

In his presence, Charity felt strength stir within her. An ember of confidence grew into a flame by the kindling of his words. As they worked side by side, the gardener shared fragments of wisdom, each one a seed planted in the soil of her mind, promising growth in due season.

The gardener pointed to a wilted sunflower that had begun to drop its seeds. "Every seed holds within it the blueprint of what it will become," he observed. "Yet without the right conditions—light, water, and nutrients—it remains only a possibility. You, Charity, are much like one of these seeds."

Charity sensed in the gardener an unparalleled wisdom. She put her fingers to her chin. "Do I have a purpose?" she asked. "A specific blueprint or… a plan I'm supposed to follow?"

"Of course," he replied. "Everyone does. But sadly, not everyone achieves the purpose for which they were created."

"How do we know what our purpose is?" she asked.

"Have you ever seen an apple tree produce lemons?"

Charity chuckled. "I don't think so."

"That's because an apple tree knows it is supposed to produce apples, and a lemon tree knows it is supposed to produce lemons. In the same way, people are designed for specific purposes. Have you ever watched a skilled mechanic repair a broken car? When someone finds their purpose, it's almost magical."

"I know what you mean," she replied. "My dad was an amazing repairman. He could fix anything that was broken."

"He found his purpose in life."

And then, a smile graced Charity's lips—a genuine reflection of joy that had long been absent.

"Joy is the most natural thing, you know," said the gardener, noticing the change in her demeanor. "It grows from the inside out and seeks the light, much like these plants do."

As Charity watched her career and marriage circle the drain, the gardener's words imparted much needed hope.

19

Charity sat on the plush carpet, her tiny fingers turning a piece of a puzzle as her mind struggled to guess its correct position in what was to become a picture of a rustic barn. At last, the puzzle piece clicked into place.

Her brother Tim sat nearby, guiding a new toy train along its path. The train chugged along its track—its wheels clicking in rhythm. In Tim's mind, it climbed the grade of a distant, snow-covered mountain. Each turn around the circuit deepened the joy on his face. The room was filled with an invisible light—the echo of Tim's mirth mingling with the scent of pine and the distant carols whispered through frosted windows.

Their brother Gary stood between the kitchen and living room, his eyes fixed on the toy train. In his gaze, a sordid flame flickered—an entitlement that seared through the innocence of the room. Shadows gathered about him, spreading discord where moments ago there had been harmony.

Then, stepping forward with the boldness of a claimant come

to collect his due, Gary's voice parted the festive air. "That's mine," he declared, the words falling heavy and hollow upon the carpeted floor.

Tim's fingers tightened around the train. His gaze flitted to Charity. In that fraction of a moment, their eyes met; a silent promise was transmitted through the bond of blood and innocence. Charity felt the weight of that look, a wordless call for help urging her into the role of protector. She unfurled from the floor, a sunflower standing tall, her slender frame casting a barrier between Tim and Gary.

"Gary," she said calmly, "the train belongs to Tim. It was given to him."

"Charity," Gary replied, "stay out of this."

The two faced each other in frozen stances. And then, it came—the point when simmering anger transformed into action. Gary shoved Tim aside and grabbed the train.

"Let go of it!" Charity yelled, trying to pry the train from Gary's hands.

Gary's fist sped through the air and connected with Charity's mouth. Her thin body tumbled backward. Her head struck the wall, and she came to rest beside the Christmas tree, unconscious. A trickle of blood ran from her mouth.

20

Charity unzipped the door to her tent. The breeze played with the loose flap, causing it to dance lightly. Inside, she slipped off her shoes and stretched her aching limbs before settling into her sleeping bag.

In the stillness, she heard a faint whisper.

"Charity…"

She sat up abruptly, her eyes scanning for the source of the intrusion. "Who's there?" she replied.

Silence answered her query, a taunting pause that stretched into the darkness. Then, with the subtlety of shadows merging into the night, the presence made itself known—Zolgreth, skulking just beyond the walls of her sanctuary.

"Charity… you cannot hide from your fate."

The words, sharp as thorns, entwined themselves around her thoughts.

"Get out!" Charity shouted.

Yet, as the whispers persisted, Zolgreth materialized from

the gloaming. "Charity," he hissed with contempt, "your efforts are but dust in the wind. All that you build, I will unmake. Your garden is a fleeting mirage," he whispered. "The flowers wilt at my passing, their beauty fading as quickly as your hope."

He circled the perimeter of the tent like a predator taunting its prey.

"Can you not feel it, Charity?" Zolgreth muttered. "You are without home, without friends, and without money." His voice grew more confident as he sensed her inner fear. "You are abandoned, forgotten by every lying friend who promised they would never forsake you."

Charity's palms pressed against her ears, trying to silence the demon's voice.

"None shall tend your wounds," he continued. Zolgreth wasn't merely attacking Charity. In her soul, fragments of her personality huddled together in a rain-soaked garden. As lightning flashed and tree limbs snapped, the young girls quivered under the weight of Zolgreth's cruel declarations.

"Abandoned," he whispered, and the word echoed through the inner garden. The girls shrank back, their eyes filled with terror. Zolgreth's voice was a gale that tore at their innocence.

"Unwanted," he said, and the soil beneath their feet crumbled.

The whispers were now a chorus of lies that blossomed into grotesque flowers of fear. Each petal revealed abandonment. The girls clutched each other, their connection a slender thread unraveling in the tempest of Zolgreth's assault.

"Unloved," the demon said, and it was as if a gale swept through the spiritual garden, bending their fragile forms to near breaking.

Charity's hands fell away from her ears, trembling at her sides as if conceding to the demon's torment. But in her heart, where the young girls lived, a plea was whispered among the storm-tossed blooms—a prayer that the dawn would banish the night.

"Unworthy," Zolgreth said, his voice penetrating the tent like a chilling breeze. His shadow stretched across the sparse interior, darkening the corners where light once lingered. The demon hovered close, his breath foul on her neck.

Charity's hands flew to her temples, pressing against them in a vain effort to silence the whispers. It was like damming a river with twigs; the flood surged, relentless and cold.

"See how easily you break?" Zolgreth asked. "Your faith is but a wisp of smoke, dispersed by the merest whisper of doubt."

Charity's spirit wilted.

"Alone," he said, the sound severing the threads that bound her to hope. Then, a small moan escaped her lips—a sound that brought glee to Zolgreth's ears.

He stepped back. A cruel smile crept across his disfigured face, the sight unseen by Charity but felt as a ripple in the air.

"Yield," he commanded softly, savoring her surrender, the culmination of his sinister work. And for a moment, Charity believed she might.

She drew her knees to her chest and wrapped her arms around them, seeking comfort in the self-made cocoon.

"Unworthy," Zolgreth said. "Forgotten."

Charity's head bowed, her hair cascading down to shield her face from unseen eyes. A tear traced a silent path along the curve of her cheek.

"Abandoned," he whispered again, the syllables a chant weaving despair into her heart.

A quiet sigh escaped her lips, not a concession but a recognition of the relentless siege. Outside, the wind raged, carrying away the last vestiges of the day. Within that gust, Zolgreth sensed his moment to retreat. He had planted seeds of desolation, and now, they needed time to germinate.

Zolgreth turned, his form blending with the shadows. As he slunk away, his presence dissolved into the ether.

21

Charity ventured from the tent toward a neglected quarter of the meadow—a place where the sun seemed reluctant to touch. The vibrant life that saturated the rest of the field was conspicuously absent here. A shiver gripped her, not from the coolness alone but from an intangible alteration in the air—a disquieting shift that whispered of things unseen.

As she walked through the tangled undergrowth, her mind entertained thoughts of both dread and intrigue. This part of the garden felt like a different realm. She sensed an oppressive weight, a pall of despair that sapped the very essence of life around her.

The decay was palpable, not just beneath her feet where leaves crumbled and rotted, but also in the sallow complexions of once proud flowers, now slumped and defeated. Charity observed the wilted greenery and noted how the plants recoiled as if burdened by a sadness that turned their petals earthward—as if viewing a manifestation of her past regrets and mistakes. The wilted foliage spoke of neglect, things left to fester and spoil without the gardener's care. In the distance, a choked gurgle of water tried to cut through the silence, but it too was trapped—ensnared by refuse that polluted its flow. There was a sorrow in that sound, a lament for the purpose it had once known.

Charity marched forward, delving deeper into the forsaken tract of land. She felt a presence just beyond the veil of sight.

A sound rose above the silence, evoking memories she had long forgotten. In the mist, she saw a small, dilapidated building near the garden's edge. Time and neglect had decayed its ivy-covered walls. The cry had come from within—a sound so laced with despair that it seemed to echo the ache of every wounded heart she had ever known.

Charity's steps slowed as she neared the structure. An empty window frame offered a glimpse inside. Peering through it, she saw a small girl curled in the corner. The girl's body seemed to flicker in the dim light as if caught between the realms of today and yesteryear. Charity stepped back reflexively, frightened by the ghostly figure. But then, compassion rose up within her. She stepped closer. "Little one," Charity called. "Why are you hiding here?"

The girl's head lifted. When her eyes met Charity's, it was as if she had peered into her own soul.

"Come out," Charity urged. "I won't hurt you."

The girl remained still.

"You're not alone," Charity whispered. "Please come out."

Charity's words, tender as a mother's embrace, seemed to dissolve into the mist. The girl shook her head. Her voice, a mere wisp of sound, crept through the vacant windowpane.

"I can't... the gardener, he'll hurt me."

A frown etched itself across Charity's brow.

"Listen to me," Charity implored. "The gardener is kind. He

would never harm you. Please believe me."

A murmur rose from the ground like a vapor, weaving through the dead foliage.

"Deceiver," the voice hissed. "He will trap you, bind you, harvest your soul."

Charity reached through the window frame as if to bridge the divide and shelter the girl from the sinister words.

"Those are lies," Charity said. "Come with me. I promise I'll keep you safe."

The girl shook her head.

Charity extended her hand, reaching toward the girl. "Look at me," she pleaded, her voice softening to a melody. "There is light beyond this darkness, hope beyond this pain. You must trust me."

But the girl stubbornly shook her head.

"You must believe me," Charity whispered, her words trailing into the chill that settled over the garden. She watched the child through the empty windowpane, her eyes a mirror of her own despair. In the stillness between them, she recognized the futility of force—the impossibility of compelling a soul so ensnared in fear and deception to embrace the unknown. The burden of what she could not change bowed Charity's shoulders. Around her, the decaying garden seemed to absorb her sorrow—its withered plants and stagnant streams commiserating with her plight.

Finally, she turned from the dilapidated building and retreated toward the center of the garden. As she walked, the girl's image haunted her—a mirror to her past—a reflection of the innocence she once knew before the world revealed its brutality. How could she abandon the child to such a fate? To do so would be to forsake herself.

Charity stepped from the cold embrace of the shadows, her feet once again finding sanctuary on the well-trodden paths of the garden. Sunlight warmed her face, dispelling the chilling gloom she had left behind.

22

Two weeks had passed since Charity had been suspended from her job. She sat in a chair opposite the wooden desk. Sunlight streamed through half-drawn blinds, casting long shadows that seemed to reach for her from the corners of the office.

The fire chief, a figure carved from years of service, sat opposite her, his gaze fixed on a manila folder—its contents a mystery. He cleared his throat, a sound carrying the weight of stones tumbling into a still pond. Charity braced herself.

"Charity," he began, his voice hinting at both regret and emotional detachment. "The results of polygraph came back."

She felt the room pivot slightly, the way the earth might shift on its axis—imperceptible yet monumental.

"Your responses indicate that you answered dishonestly regarding the allegations of taking the narcotics," he said, his eyes finally meeting hers. "The results suggest you know more than you've admitted to."

Charity blinked, trying to control her outward appearance.

"Is there anything you wish to say?" he asked.

Disbelief encompassed her mind, her heart plummeting as if caught in the downdraft of a helicopter's blades.

"Charity," the chief continued, his voice cold, "I have no choice but to terminate your employment effective immediately."

Scenes flashed before Charity's eyes. Dangling from a rope on a rain-drenched cliff, she fitted a man with a rescue harness and then guided him slowly upward as an unseen crew above hauled up his safety line. Cradling a newborn baby, she fought her way through waist-deep snow, struggling to reach the warmth of a waiting ambulance. Kneeling beside a man pinned between the bumper of a car and a guardrail. She cried as the man asked if he would be okay. She lied, telling him he would be fine, knowing he was about to take his last breath. One scene after another paraded through her mind, a highlight reel of her best and worst moments.

"Please understand, this is never easy," the chief said, his tone trying to approximate sympathy. "But the evidence leaves us with little room for leniency."

Charity heard his words as though from afar. She stood at the junction of two worlds—one familiar, bright with the blaze of flashing lights and the camaraderie of shared danger—the other, a dark realm where shadowy figures whisper of betrayal and loss.

She rested her hands in her lap, her calm facade a mask sculpted by years of emotionally detaching herself from gruesome scenes while making life-or-death decisions. Her composure did not crack even now as the chief's words hung in the air. She fixed her gaze on a nondescript point over his shoulder, focusing on the rhythm of her breathing, determined to maintain self-control.

"You'll need to return your department-issued gear by the end of the week." The chief's voice held the indifferent tone of procedural necessity, yet to Charity, each syllable clattered against the walls of her soul like chains being dragged across stone.

Charity nodded. "Of course, Chief," she said at last.

She rose from her chair and turned toward the door, the whisper of her pants brushing against the chair fabric sounding unnaturally loud in the charged silence. The door swung open with a soft creak. She walked into the hall, her presence diminishing with each step as if she were becoming a ghost in her own story. The linoleum, worn smooth by the passage of countless feet rushing to answer the call of duty, now bore her solitary steps.

Charity arrived at the main entrance to the station and stepped outside. Walking toward the parking lot, her thoughts tangled into knots of confusion and despair; how could her career have ended so abruptly?

She reached her car and retrieved her keys. With a click, the doors unlocked, and she slipped inside—the enclosed space a temporary refuge from the glaring scrutiny of the world beyond its windows.

In the solitude of her sedan, Charity allowed herself to cry over the implosion of her life's work. Her phone announced a new voice message. Her hand, unsteady, retrieved her phone from her purse. As her thumb hovered over the button, trepidation filled her mind. What news awaited her? With a button press, she braced herself against the tide of words soon to wash over her.

"Charity, it's Brad Langdon. I wish I had better news, but I've received the paperwork for your husband's divorce filing. There are several recommendations I need to discuss with you regarding your response and potential settlement options."

Charity's heart imploded. A single, bitter laugh escaped her. Divorce. The word was anathema to her. She had vowed she would never use it, either as a threat to someone else or to describe her intentions. She had known her marriage was fraying—the love she had once known was replaced by silence and mistrust. Yet, she hoped her relationship with Michael could be restored. The abruptness of its ending delivered a punch she hadn't braced for.

"Please call me back at your earliest convenience," the attorney concluded.

As the message ended, Charity sat still. Her gaze drifted beyond the windshield, where the world moved in its relentless rhythm. The dissolution of her marriage was the final anchor giving way in the storm; a promised safe harbor that had silently rotted beneath the waves, weakened by neglect, until it disintegrated. Charity closed her eyes. In the darkness, she saw the shimmering strands of her once woven-together life unraveling.

23

Charity's eyes opened to the glow of dawn caressing the tent's walls. Her mind, still tethered to the fabric of sleep, could not immediately place the vague sense of concern. Then, like a gentle breeze carrying distant melodies, the scents of bacon and coffee wafted into the tent. An alarm went off inside her as she wondered who was cooking food outside. Her fingers fumbled with the sleeping bag's zipper, the metal teeth yielding to her haste as daylight spilled into her refuge.

She tore open the tent door to see a man crouched by a small fire, his hands tending to the flames. The man's sapphire eyes lifted to meet hers. His gaze did not waver, nor did it pierce. In his presence, Charity felt the weight of her anxiety lift like shadows retreating before the advance of dawn. Yet, she remained still, unable to reconcile the peace he exuded with the unease that had roused her from slumber.

"Good morning," he called out.

"Who are you?" Charity asked, her gaze locked onto his eyes, searching for an intent that might betray his serene features.

The crackle of the fire hushed, awaiting his response. "They call me Joshua," he said with a smile. "I'm the gardener's son."

Charity took an involuntary step back.

"Please, join me for breakfast," he said, motioning toward the modest spread near the fire.

"Is that bacon?" Charity asked.

"Yes, and coffee."

With each cautious step toward the warmth of the fire, she wrestled with suspicion on the one hand and an inexplicable trust on the other.

"Thank you," she said softly. As she approached, she observed him—the way his hands moved with purpose, how his presence seemed to weave tranquility into the air.

He offered her a cup of coffee. She accepted and raised the mug to her lips, the warm liquid cascading into the depths of her body. Joshua stirred the embers of the fire, and the flames leaped up as if to listen in on their conversation.

"Tell me, Charity," he said, "what troubles you?"

She hesitated. It wasn't just the question but how he asked it—as if he already knew the weight of her sorrows but invited her to share them anyway.

"I feel… lost," she admitted. "I have no home, no job, and now… my marriage might be over."

Joshua listened, his eyes reflecting compassion. "Yet here you are," he observed.

The worry on her face gave way to a smile. "I feel like I'm here for a reason," she mused. "Some divine purpose that isn't clear yet."

"And what do you think that purpose might be?" he asked.

"A lot of strange things have happened since I first came

here," she replied, "I don't think they are coincidences. I met the gardener and it seemed like suddenly, my life had purpose. Then, I lost my job and my house. And my husband asked for a divorce. It's like…"

"You're in a war?" Joshua said, finishing her sentence.

"Exactly."

"What do you think the war is about?" he asked.

Charity stared in his eyes that flickered with a cobalt fire. "Part of it seems to be about my past. I had a dream where my brother beat the crap out of me. And then," she continued slowly, "I beat the tar out of drunk guy at a bus stop. I don't remember doing it, but a friend watched the whole thing. I don't understand what's happening."

"How old were you when your brother beat you?"

"Maybe ten years old," she replied.

"Have you met the little girl that lives in the building over there?" he asked, gesturing to the perimeter of the garden.

"You know about her?"

He smiled. "I know all the inhabitants of the garden."

"She needs help," Charity said, her voice a plea of desperation.

"Together, perhaps we can help her."

"We need to hurry," Charity said anxiously.

Joshua rose and began walking toward the shadows that encompassed the desolate quadrant of the garden. Charity set down her coffee mug and followed him. As they neared the edge of the property, the dilapidated building became visible in the distance. Its windows were like the eyes of a soul that had seen too much; its doors sealed forbidden secrets. She felt the pull, the undeniable connection between her fragmented heart and the girl trapped within those walls.

Charity stopped. "I tried to get her to leave, but she refused."

"Almost as if she preferred being there?" Joshua asked.

"Yes," she said. "But why? Why would she choose to remain there?" Joshua looked at the building and then at Charity. "Have you ever known someone who was miserable, but refused to take action to change their circumstance?"

"So, it's a self-imposed prison?" Charity asked, recognition spreading across her face. "How could such a place be of her own making?"

"*Your own making.*" Joshua corrected her.

"I knew it!" she said. "That's why I'm here. That girl…" The words came forth like the breaking of dawn. "She's a part of me."

"A wounded part of your soul," he said. "Living in a prison built out of pain, by malevolent spirits masquerading as protectors, fortified by lies told so often they are mistaken for truth."

Charity stood silent.

"She is held there by the power of deception. The power of lies. She believes she is safe. The only way to set her free is to convince her she is not safe. You must show her that true safety lies outside of her prison."

"But how do I do that?" Charity asked.

"You must gain her trust."

"Trust," Charity repeated the word as she walked toward the building, with Joshua following her.

"You can do it," Joshua said. "Your voice must be the lighthouse guiding her through the storm."

She felt their presence before seeing them—dark spirits, their shadowy shapes darting at the edges of her vision.

"You have no power here," a voice said.

Charity touched the building and peered through a window pane. "My child," Charity said, ignoring the demonic presence, "I am here for you."

"Keep calling to her," Joshua whispered.

"Sweet child, listen to me," Charity continued. "You may feel safe here, but I know your pain. I only want you to be healed."

A sound punctured the silence—a rustling, followed by the creak of a hinge. A door swung open, revealing the girl's haunting face.

"Come out," Charity urged.

Intrigued by the invitation, the girl peered out. Seeing Joshua, recognition flickered across her face—a distant memory of warmth, safety, and light.

"Are you afraid?" he asked gently.

Her body trembled, not with fear, but with awe. Slowly, she extended a hand and took a tentative step, her gaze anchored to the kindness radiating from Joshua.

"Freedom feels strange," he said, kneeling to meet her eye level. "But you'll grow to like it."

Charity silently watched the girl's lips form a hesitant smile. In the newfound courage reflected in those young eyes, Charity recognized the dawning of trust—a fragile present perched in the light of possibility.

Joshua extended his hand, palm up, toward the girl, who stood trembling. "I see your wounds," he said softly. "Let me help you heal them."

Hesitation flickered in her eyes—old fears wrestling with the promise of healing. Yet, as the warmth of his gaze wrapped around her like a gentle embrace, the girl placed her small, scarred hand in his.

Joshua looked at a wound on the girl's face. "I see betrayal," he said. "Can I remove it?"

The girl nodded. Joshua held his hand over the scar and gradually, it faded until it was gone. "How do you feel?"

A smile appeared on her face. "Better!"

Next, he pointed to a wound on her abdomen. "Can I remove your anger?"

"Yes."

He placed his hand on the wound and in a minute, it too was gone.

"How do you feel?"

"Happy!" she said with a wide smile.

Joshua continued the process, identifying wounds, asking if he could heal them, and assessing the results. Charity watched. Tears welled up in her eyes as the girl's face transformed under the tenderness of his touch. Her pale skin regained the soft glow of innocence. Once dull with bitterness, her eyes sparkled with the first glimmers of hope.

"Your heart has been a battlefield," Joshua said, "But the war is over now. It is time for peace. I would like to make you whole again."

As he spoke, the girl looked at Charity with wonder and confusion. Charity, too, felt the stirrings of uncertainty.

"Both of you have journeyed alone," he explained, "But you were designed to be one. It's time to be united and live together.

"But how? How do we become one again?" Charity asked.

"Now that she has been healed," Joshua said to Charity, "it's safe for me to reunite you."

"Will it hurt?" the girl asked.

"Not at all," he replied.

"Then let's begin," Charity said.

"I want you to hold each other's hands and close your eyes," he instructed them.

Obediently, Charity closed her eyes. The girl did the same, and their hands clasped.

"Envision your hearts beating as one," he continued, "filled with love for the other."

In her mind, Charity determined she would love the girl, regardless of her faults. As she did, they began to merge.

"Embrace each other's pain as your own," he whispered. "Let love transform the pain."

A gentle tide washed over Charity, carrying away shards of old wounds.

"Forgive," he said.

Tears gathered behind Charity's closed eyes, not of sorrow but of release.

"Forgive," she repeated.

The merging was imperceptible, like the slow dawning of day when night recedes so seamlessly that one cannot pinpoint the exact moment of transition. Charity sensed the girl's essence intertwine with hers.

"Open your eyes," came Joshua's command.

When Charity looked upon the world again, she viewed it through a lens polished by love and forgiveness. The girl was no longer present, at least not physically. But she felt the child's presence internally as if an inner re-alignment had occurred.

24

The library smelled of paper and sanitizer. Charity sat at one of the public computer terminals near the windows, her coat draped across the back of the chair. Outside, the sky pressed low—gray and spitting mist—but the soft hum of printers and distant footsteps made the place feel almost safe.

She stared at the login screen.

It took her three tries to remember her password for the job search site.

The screen loaded. Rows of listings appeared.

Paramedic.

EMT.

Private transport.

Dispatch.

She scrolled past them all. The tension in her shoulders deepened. She still had the certifications. The hours. The field experience. But something inside her recoiled at the thought of climbing back into a rig. It wasn't fear—it was knowing. Knowing what it would cost. Knowing what it took from her, piece by piece, until her soul had become a trauma room—always triaging, but never healing.

She clicked into a listing anyway.

Phlebotomist – American Red Cross (Seattle Chapter)
Mobile donor services. Statewide travel. Must be comfortable driving a medical van, managing supplies, performing blood draws, and recording data. Full-time, early mornings and weekends required.

Charity read the rest of the posting. She could do it. Easily. The pay wasn't great, but it would cover her bills. And in some strange way, it almost made sense—drawing blood instead of watching it spill. Serving without being first on scene.

She closed the tab.

It wasn't the work that bothered her—it was the drive. She liked driving. But the job would have her driving across the entire state. Sometimes getting up at 4am and ending her shift after dark. No home. No anchor. The van would become her house, the donor chairs would be her only conversations.

She logged out of the session, then stood, and headed toward the exit. Outside, she turned and began the short walk to her favorite hangout. The Bayside Coffee Shop was located three blocks east of the library. She didn't know if it was the smell of espresso or the way the light came through the front windows, but something about the place made her feel tethered.

She opened the door and stepped inside. Charity hovered near the entrance watching the barista behind the counter as he chatted with a customer, his voice warm but never pushy. He slid a drink across the counter and gave a nod of genuine thanks.

Charity's eyes lingered.

I could do that.

She didn't mean forever. Just… for now. Something small.

Something that didn't involve life or death decisions.

A counter.

A rhythm.

A place where she could hear her own thoughts without being drowned in sirens or swallowed by silence.

25

The fire crackled softly, its glow casting golden ribbons across the surrounding stones. Joshua knelt beside it, coaxing heat from the coals with the reverence of a priest tending a sacred flame. The skillet hissed as oil met flesh—fish freshly caught from the stream that wound beneath the Garden's northern arch.

He worked in silence, but his thoughts were not still.

She would come.

He had felt her soul stirring the air—an internal shift, subtle but sure, like leaves turning color before the first frost. The kind of shift that only comes when courage begins to overtake fear.

She's tired, he surmised. *But she's still coming.*

He reached for the earthen pot of potatoes and adjusted its position above the flame. His hands moved with practiced grace, but his mind remained on her. Charity. The one who walked with open arms and hidden wounds. The one who fought. The one who wept.

The Garden had waited for her—its vines tangled, its soil

brittle. But now it pulsed with expectancy. The earth hummed beneath his feet.

He looked toward a barely perceptible path that led toward darkness—a place between worlds where screams were frozen. A dozen times today, he had glanced toward it. Not out of worry, but love. The kind of love that waits without demand.

"She still doubts," he whispered, "but her heart is beginning to remember."

Joshua pulled the skillet from the fire and set two plates upon a stone beside him. The wind stirred gently. Crickets began their chorus. Somewhere nearby, the owl gave its call.

And then— The gravel stirred.

He stood, slowly, his frame silhouetted in the growing dusk. Not with urgency. Not with surprise. But with quiet joy.

She was here.

26

Charity's car rolled to a stop, the crunch of gravel under tires giving way to silence as she cut the engine. She stepped out into the waning light of late afternoon. Exiting the car, she walked toward the campfire that crackled beyond her tent, where the blue-eyed man tended to a skillet over the flames.

"Joshua?" Charity called out.

"Charity," he replied, turning to greet her. "I hoped you'd return before dusk."

As she approached the fire, the scent of broiling fish caused her stomach to growl. She moved closer to the blaze, drawn by its movement as much as by the man who tended it. She watched Joshua adjust a blackened pot over the flames.

"Joshua," Charity said, her voice low as if she were afraid to disrupt the tranquility of the evening. "This process… the healing process—it's like wrestling with shadows. How can I be healed of things I'm not aware of?"

He handed her a plate. "Eat and we'll talk."

She accepted his offer; the warmth of the earthenware seeped into her palms.

"Charity," he began, his eyes reflecting the fire's dance, "the healing you need is manifold; it's deeper than the wounds you feel right now."

A forkful of potato paused midway to her lips, her hand trembling slightly. "What do you mean?" she asked, her voice lost in the crackle of the fire.

"Within you reside fragments, each one crying out for healing. They are parts of your soul, traumatized, each one holding onto moments of despair from your past."

"How… how many are there?" The question emerged, choked by the fear of knowing too much.

"More than we have uncovered," he replied.

Charity saw her broken soul spread out before her—a ravaged landscape she had traversed in ignorance.

"So, there are more," she said, "Does this mean another game of hide and seek?"

"Seek and you shall find," Joshua replied. "Many people are afraid of what they might find, so they never seek."

"I'll admit, I'm a little afraid of what I might find."

"Do you trust me?" Joshua asked.

"Part of me trusts you completely," she replied, "but the other part—the one that's been burned—it doesn't trust you yet."

"Double-mindedness," he said softly, "when one part of your soul disagrees with another part."

Charity considered his words as she ate. Finally, she spoke. "Do you think double-mindedness can keep me from my destiny? What I mean is, if one part of my soul wants to pursue a certain career, but another part resists, would it keep me from doing what I'm destined to do?"

"What do you think?"

"I think there's another little girl inside me that doesn't trust God. And I think I need to find her and have a little chat," Charity said, grinning.

Joshua rose. "Come with me," he said, extending a hand to help her up.

She placed her hand in his and stood up. There was a part of her that wanted to flee, to deny the existence of her hidden pain. Yet another part—emboldened by Joshua's presence—yearned to face these concealed fragments, to acknowledge them, and if possible, to heal them.

"Where are we going?" she asked.

"You'll see in a minute," he said, teasing her curiosity.

With a nod, Charity followed. The meal lay forgotten behind them. Ahead lay the uncharted territories of her soul. They followed a narrow path that wound through the heart of the garden, then Joshua led her toward a forest. A massive arch appeared flanked by a stone wall. They passed beneath it and descended a hill, the rustle of their steps mingling with the nocturnal chorus of crickets and the distant hoot of an owl. It was in this contemplative silence that Charity first heard them—the soft, heartrending sobs that seemed to come from the earth beneath her feet.

"Can you hear their cries?" Joshua asked.

Charity nodded, her heart welling with empathy for the suffering she sensed but could not yet see. "Who are they?"

"Parts of you—long forgotten and yearning for freedom."

As they approached a stone building at the bottom of the hill, the cries grew more distinct. The structure loomed before them, its walls gray and somber, holding within it the echoes of lost innocence.

"Love is the key," Joshua said, touching the cold stone door that stood between them and the weeping within.

Charity stepped forward, her resolve hardening like the stones beneath her feet. She reached out, pressing her palm against the door. "I'm here now. You're not alone," she said. "I know you're scared, but I promise to protect you."

The door creaked open. "Come," Charity said. "You don't have to hide any longer." A band of little girls emerged from behind the door.

Joshua motioned for them to come near. One by one, the girls approached him. He addressed each one in turn, asking permission to remove their sorrow, shame, guilt, anger, fear, or abandonment. His hands glowed with an otherworldly luminescence as he healed each wound.

After each girl had been healed, Joshua helped them extend forgiveness and love while embracing Charity's pain as their own. As they held hands, each one became a part of her. With each healing and integration, she felt the dungeon within her crumbling, the chains of past torment falling away, and the garden—her garden—blossoming anew beneath the rising moon's light.

27

Charity lay still on the tent floor as a deluge of memories flooded her mind. Unbidden and unwelcome, they swept over her with the ferocity of a tempest. She was back at the fire station; the smell of burnt rubber was heavy in the air. The radio crackled with urgency, dispatching her to the scene of a catastrophic highway pile-up.

Her heart raced as she surveyed the chaos—shattered glass glinting like ice under the harsh glare of floodlights, the wail of sirens, and desperate cries for help. She knelt beside an overturned car, the jaws of life prying open a mangled door to reveal a man trapped inside, his lifeblood draining away.

"Stay with me," she said, her hands drenched with blood. The moment the man's spirit slipped away, she felt a whisper of departure that left a void in its wake. Her mind rehearsed past failures. She clutched her head, trying in vain to block the images. "Please," she cried, the word dissolving into the ether. The echo of the man's final heartbeat pounded in her ears.

"Charity," a voice hissed, "you couldn't save him."

The words tormented her. "Useless to those who lay dying... just like you were to your husband," Zolgreth said.

"I'm not useless. You're a liar!" she countered, her words scattered by the wind as doubt crept through her defenses.

"Remember how you failed?" The demon searched her memories, conjuring in her mind more visions of grief—a cinema filled with lost lives. "How many people died because of your decisions?" he asked, sensing the fractures in her spirit. "Let go. There is no gardener to tend to your brokenness."

"Leave me alone," she cried. But the malevolent whispers grew louder and more insistent, threatening to drown her.

A sudden jolt of anguish pierced through the fog of her mind as another vision assailed her. She saw herself standing before Michael—the man she had once vowed to love forever, his eyes as cold as the words he hurled at her. "Why did I ever trust you?" he said. The ring that once symbolized their love lay discarded on the ground. The scene played out before her, as vivid as the day it unfolded, tearing open wounds she thought had long since scarred over.

"Is this what you wanted? You are bound by chains of your own making. Where is your strength now?" Zolgreth asked. "What worth do you have if you can't save others? You can't even save yourself. Where is your God?"

Her eyes closed gently.

"Surrender," he demanded. "Let go."

Charity lay motionless, her spirit a fragment of the woman who had courageously faced infernos. Beneath the cloak of night, she lay frozen as though carved from a slab of stone, her features etched with the tools of a battle fought in the hidden realm of the spirit. But the stillness that gripped her was not the precursor to an end. Rather, it was the deep breath taken before the plunge, the hush that befalls the forest before the fury of an approaching storm. In the stillness, Charity teetered between succumbing to the forces of darkness and rising anew.

28

Charity stood alone near the edge of the garden. The light was soft—end-of-day golden—but she didn't feel its warmth.

The soil beneath her was rich and well-watered. Her hands, by contrast, felt cold.

She looked down at her palms, flexing her fingers slowly. They had done so much. Held the dying. Cradled the living. Carefully inserted needles, wrapped bandages, and pushed medications into veins, sometimes without knowing for sure if the IV line would hold.

Sometimes, it hadn't.

She clenched her fists and sat on a bench near an oak tree, her head bowing forward, her elbows on her knees.

She hadn't spoken of it since it happened.

Not to Travis.

Not to Joshua.

Not even in prayer.

Because she didn't want forgiveness.

She wanted—she *deserved* punishment.

The gardener approached. He moved without sound, his hands still dusted with soil from his work. He sat beside her but didn't speak.

Charity finally did.

"There was a call," she said, "A man… congestive heart failure. Pretty bad. He couldn't breathe. We were barely keeping him upright. I got an IV—kind of. I told myself it was a good line. I told Travis it was in. I pushed the Lasix."

She stared into the grass.

"But the IV wasn't patent," she said. "It was infiltrated from the start. I saw the swelling around the catheter. That's why he got worse, and then coded."

The gardener didn't move.

"I lied," she said. "I knew it was a bad line. I should have started another one, but I didn't. Because I couldn't admit it. Not in front of Travis."

She looked down at her hands again. "I killed him," she said finally, tears falling from her eyes. "My stupid pride."

The gardener reached for her hand but didn't take it. He let his palm rest open between them.

"I have buried many things," he said softly. "But the hardest to bury are the things my children refuse to release."

Charity's shoulders trembled. "I'm not asking you to make it okay."

"I wouldn't," he replied. "Because it wasn't okay."

She sniffled.

"But I will tell you this," he added, "you cannot carry this burden forever."

Charity didn't hear Joshua approaching. But when she looked up, he was there—silently watching them.

"You think it was your hands that failed him," Joshua said, walking slowly toward her.

"They did," she replied bitterly.

Joshua knelt before her.

"Charity," he said, "your hands did not hold his life. I did."

She opened her mouth to argue, but the words wouldn't form.

"You think if the IV had been perfect, the outcome would've been different. Maybe. Maybe not. But you've turned that moment into a courtroom—and made yourself the judge, jury, and executioner."

Her lip quivered. "I didn't mean to lie."

"You meant to save him. You made a flawed choice under unbearable pressure. And then you punished yourself for not being perfect."

Joshua reached up and touched her face—right where the tear was forming. "Your guilt doesn't honor his life. It only chains yours."

Charity looked up. "But I knew better."

Joshua's hand dropped to her shoulder. "Then let that knowledge become wisdom for the future—not torment over your past. Guilt will never teach you what grace can. You've forgiven others. Now, you must forgive yourself."

She broke then.

Fully.

No restraint.

No hiding.

Just sobbing.

Joshua pulled her into his arms.

Not to fix her.

Not to reason.

Just to hold her.

When the trembling had slowed, he whispered into her hair, "I saw you. In that truck. In that moment. I never turned away from you. And I never will."

29

Charity's eyes fluttered open. She pushed back the covers. Rising from her makeshift bed, she stepped out of the tent. The garden greeted her, a splash of color and life sprawling before her. Dewdrops adorned each leaf and petal. The air hummed with the songs of early birds heralding the dawn.

Charity ventured deeper into the garden than she had gone before. Then, she noticed the sunflowers—their faces turned east toward the morning sun, standing guard over a hidden corner of the garden. From behind them, the old man emerged.

"Good morning, Charity," the man said, his voice rich with warmth. "The dawn is waiting for you."

A broad smile graced her face. "Morning," she replied.

"Come, walk with me," he beckoned, gesturing toward an archway adorned with flowers she could not name.

Charity followed, the rustle of leaves underfoot. They passed the familiar beds of flowers and then moved into territory unmarked by her footprints. The gardener matched his pace to hers, an unhurried amble that allowed the silence to speak as loudly as their words.

"Tell me, Charity," the gardener began, breaking the comfortable quiet between them, "what stirs in your heart this morning?"

"I think there are spirits tormenting me… even while I sleep."

"Ah." He nodded. "The garden is a battlefield. Flowers strive to fulfill their purpose, but weeds and insects attack them. Strong plants can resist these attacks and flourish, but weak ones will wither and die."

"So, whether we die or prosper is determined by our strength?"

"Precisely," the gardener said. "There is no way to avoid attacks. The sun shines and the rain falls equally on all living creatures. It is what a plant chooses to do with the rain and sun it receives that determines whether it lives or dies."

As they walked, Charity felt the layers of her guarded heart peel back, petal by petal, revealing the rawness beneath. Yet in the presence of the gardener, the ache felt less like an open wound and more like fertile ground.

"Charity, you've transported many people who have committed suicide, haven't you?"

"More than I want to remember."

"Have any of their circumstances been so dire that if you were in their shoes, you would have taken your life?"

"I don't think so," she said.

"Why does one person succumb to despair and hopelessness while another finds a way to get through it?"

"I guess some people are made of tougher stuff."

"And how does one become tough?" the gardener asked with a grin.

"By persevering through difficult times," she said confidently.

"And now we've come full circle."

Charity followed the gardener, her feet treading a path concealed by the overhanging leaves of ferns and grasses. They emerged into a clearing where sunlight pooled like liquid gold, bathing everything in a gentle radiance that seemed to pulse with the very heartbeat of creation. She paused to gaze upon flowers in hues more vibrant than any painter's palette.

"Beautiful, isn't it?" he said.

"More than words can say," Charity replied, her mouth hanging open in astonishment.

In this secluded corner, Charity felt the weight of her burdens begin to lift. The shadows in her heart receded, edged away by the light that now seeped through every pore of her being. She breathed freely for the first time in what felt like an eternity.

"Take your time," the gardener said.

And Charity did just that, immersing herself in the sacred silence, allowing the divinity of the space to fill the hollow places within her.

"Every heart harbors its own garden. Just as we nurture these flowers and trees, so must we tend to the flora within us."

Charity listened intently.

"See how the lilies bend toward the light?" He gestured to the radiant blooms that glowed with an inner luminescence. "They seek what gives them life. Yet weeds, they thrive in neglect, spreading where care is absent."

His words painted a picture in Charity's mind—each virtue a blossoming flower, each failing a choking weed.

"Within you," he continued, "lies a garden yearning for attention. Weeds may take root when light is scarce, and so it is with the spirit."

The image of the garden—a mirror to her soul's landscape—became more apparent. Charity recognized the brambles of rejection and the thistles of fear that had, over time and through neglect, been woven into her being.

"Discouragement," Charity said, "it's like ivy. It clings and climbs and suffocates."

"Indeed," the gardener agreed. "Even the most persistent weeds wilt before a gardener's loving hand. It is not the presence of darkness but the lack of light that allows despair to flourish."

Charity's heart, long shrouded in despair's creeping vines, beat with renewed vigor as she listened.

"Tell me how," she replied.

"Ah," he said, "In the same way you would tend this garden, you must tend to the welfare of your soul. The weeds of the soul are things like fear, anger, resentment, self-doubt, rejection, hatred, and despair. If you let them grow in the garden of your heart, they will choke out the things you need to prosper—love, hope, faith, joy, courage, and compassion.

Charity stared at a patch of ground and began pulling up weeds and tossing them aside.

"If you leave them there, in time, they will root again. Why don't you give them to me?"

She handed the weeds to the old man, who examined them, and then held one up. "Bitterness," he said softly.

Charity froze. It dawned on her that she was not merely giving him weeds but the emotions that kept her in bondage. She pulled another weed and handed it to the gardener. "I'm giving you my anger," she said. She pulled up another weed. "I'm giving you my fear." She uprooted a thorn. "Here, take my hatred."

"And why are you doing that?"

"Because all they do is hold me back," she said, sobbing.

"Any time you feel an emotion that you don't want, treat it like a weed. Pull it out and give it to me."

Charity nodded with understanding; her heart buoyed with the expectation of healing. With every word from the gardener, she felt the grip of her inner demons loosen their hold.

With the deliberateness of one who understood the sacredness of beginnings, the gardener knelt, his knees imprinting the soft earth. He retrieved a single seed from within the folds of his worn jacket. It was small and unassuming, yet held within it a promise greater than its size.

"Here, Charity," he said. His outstretched hand offered the seed to her like a sacrament.

Charity extended her hand with her palm upturned. The seed, placed delicately upon her skin, seemed to pulse with potential. The gardener's hands closed around hers. "Plant this in the soil," he said. "Let your intentions be the water, your perseverance be the sun, and your faith the fertile ground."

The soil was cool and yielding beneath her touch, accepting her fingers as they carved a small cradle for the seed. Charity carefully nestled the seed into its earthen bed.

There was something deeply elemental about the action, as if by giving life to this seed, she was nurturing the dormant parts of her soul, coaxing them toward the light after years in shadow.

"Good," the gardener said with a nod. "Now we wait, we watch, and we tend to it. Growth is a journey, not an end."

Charity picked up a watering can and held it with both hands. Water cascaded onto the soil, soaking in around the freshly planted seed. Droplets splashed lightly against her fingers. She watched, fascinated by how the earth darkened, accepting the nourishment with silent gratitude.

"Care is constant, like the flow of water," the gardener said, standing beside her. "It's not just about quenching thirst; it's about releasing love and developing the patience to see things grow."

30

Charity huddled within the fragile sanctuary of her tent, the walls quaking with each violent caress of the wind. She clung to her sleeping bag—in an attempt to keep the cold rain from seeping through the layers of her clothing. Once a peaceful sanctuary, the garden outside had been transformed into a war zone.

The rain commenced its assault, a deluge descending upon her flimsy refuge. At that moment, a flash of lightning split the sky. Charity's gaze fell upon the silhouette of a tree.

The wind roared in defiance. The nylon walls of the tent billowed and snapped violently. Lightning ripped through the night sky, striking a nearby tree. Charity hunched down as splinters and bark peppered the tent like shrapnel fired from the heavens. The scent of ozone and sap filled the air.

With the next gust, the tent shook violently. Charity inventoried her options with clinical detachment. To remain was to court fate; to flee was to brave the unknown fury outside. She decided to leave before the tent was destroyed. "Guide me," she asked, a prayer for divine direction.

She opened the door of the tent and darted through the gap. The storm greeted her with a slap of wind, a baptism by fury, her hair lashing about her like whips. She squinted through the veil of rain, searching for the outline of her car. Her shoes sank into the mire, anchoring her momentarily in the sodden earth. With a grunt, she freed herself.

She could feel it—the storm's apex had arrived, raging against her with a fury that felt personal, as if Satan himself sought to drive her back into the jaws of despair.

Charity moved forward, her eyes narrowing against torrents of rain. Her car—a faint silhouette shrouded in the curtain of water—beckoned from the gravel driveway.

The waterlogged earth attempted to claim her with every step, but she persisted. Finally reaching the car, Charity fumbled with shaking hands to find the keys in the pocket of her coat. The lock yielded, and she slipped inside, the door closing with a thud. Safe within the metal cocoon, she leaned back against the seat, her breathing slowing, her clothes clinging to her skin.

The storm asserted its claim to supremacy. Plants that once stood as sentinels of serenity now writhed in agony, their stems bending to the will of the wind. But inside, the stillness allowed Charity to close her eyes and seek solace in the silent company of her thoughts.

31

The next morning

Charity stepped out of her car, still soaking wet. She stood still, momentarily conducting a battle damage assessment. The storm had passed, but its wrath was etched in the scene before her. The once orderly rows of vibrant flora were now a tangle of broken stems and uprooted blooms. Leaves, branches, and petals lay strewn across the muddy earth like casualties of war.

As she took in the destruction, two figures appeared. The gardener, his hands as rugged as the bark on the trees he tended, walked with a steady grace that belied the havoc around him. Beside him was Joshua with a brown bag in his hands.

"This will take time to clean up," he observed, "but first, we should eat."

Charity smiled in agreement.

Joshua gathered sticks and stones, carefully placing them with a handful of dry twigs that he produced from his pocket. He struck a match against a stone and ignited the kindling. The fire caught quickly, its glow chasing away the remnants of darkness clinging to dawn's edge. Charity watched as he worked the flames, coaxing them into a temple of warmth and light. The aroma of food unfolded, intermingling with the damp, loamy scent of the earth.

Charity settled close to the fire. The gardener looked at her. "You know," he began, his voice carrying the weight of gentle authority, "this garden is not unlike us—vulnerable to the storms that pass, yet resilient in ways we often forget."

Charity listened while eating. The gardener pointed toward the expanse of upturned earth and shattered flora. "It absorbs the rain, the wind, the lightning… and still it endures. Still, it grows. Like the human soul," he continued, locking eyes with Charity, "we bear our tempests within, the howl of our fears and the deluge of our sorrows. But there is redemption for us. There is strength in our roots that we only discover when faced with the devastation of our storms."

Charity felt in her heart the truth of his analogy. Tattered by battle, her soul yearned for the same restoration she understood the garden needed. With each word the gardener spoke, the seed of hope planted deep within her was nurtured, and she sensed the first stirrings of growth amid the ruins of her inner world.

The fire crackled, punctuating the silence that followed, and for a moment, all that existed was the trio, the flame, and the promise of healing.

Charity gazed at the gardener, his hands resting on an old, gnarled walking stick, his fingers tracing the wood's whorls as if reading braille. He spoke of rebirth, his voice a soft cadence riding the morning air.

"This garden," he said, "will bloom anew. As we toil and tend these beds, so too shall we nurture our spirits."

The gardener rose and Charity followed him. He knelt beside

a flowerbed choked with debris, clearing away broken branches, revealing the tender shoots beneath. "Every sprout, every leaf is a tale of endurance," he said, lifting a stem cradling a single unopened bud.

Charity watched, her senses attuned to his methodical movements—how he tended to the wounded earth as if whispering a prayer with each touch.

He turned and walked several paces then stopped. "Here," he gestured toward a section of the garden where wildflowers once swayed in the breeze, now trampled and forlorn. "They need space to breathe, space to be free from the weight of the wreckage."

Near the edge of the ravaged garden, Joshua walked toward the crumpled frame of Charity's tent. A large limb that had fallen in the storm lay atop the tent. Charity stepped forward, her shoes sinking slightly into the softened soil as she approached Joshua and reached out to help him. He nodded, and together, they lifted, moving the branch to the edge of the clearing.

"Does it ever get easier?" Charity asked as they set down the timber. "The healing, I mean."

"Each scar tells a story," he answered. "And with each story, there is learning. With learning, comes ease."

She brushed a lock of hair from her eyes. "Sometimes I fear the scars are too deep," she said nervously.

"Even the deepest wounds will find closure, if you're willing to pursue the healing process to its conclusion." he assured her, picking up a branch that lay at their feet. "When healing doesn't happen, it's because we've given up. The key is persistence."

She watched as he removed debris from around a cluster of crushed flowers. There was a certainty in his actions that made her believe, if only for a moment, that healing and restoration was not just possible but inevitable.

"Thank you," Charity said, "for believing in my healing, even when I can't see it."

"Faith is not about sight. It's about holding on to the truth in the midst of darkness, trusting that the light will prevail."

32

Charity closed the door and took a seat in the office of Brad Langdon, her attorney.

"Mrs. McBride," he began, "thank you for coming."

"Of course," Charity replied. "Thank you for seeing me."

"Let's get straight to the point," he said, leaning forward slightly, his eyes fixed upon hers. "The charge against you is not terribly serious. Fourth degree assault with no prior convictions usually carries a sentence of six months to a year of probation."

Charity nodded. "I understand," she replied anxiously, "but I'm innocent. I didn't assault anyone."

Mr. Langdon peered over his glasses, inspecting the purple bruises on her knuckles. "And these?" he inquired, nodding toward her hands.

Charity's face flushed, but she remained silent.

"Mrs. McBride," he continued, his tone empathetic. "The courts tend to favor victims in assault cases. I've read the police report and I've seen the photos of your husband. They are compelling evidence suggesting he was assaulted. In my opinion, you do not want to bring this case before a jury."

"I know things look bad," Charity said, "but I swear I did not harm Michael. We had an argument. I left the house. He followed me and when he was outside, he slipped on a patch of ice and hit his face on the sidewalk. When he called 911, he told them I hit him."

Langdon listened patiently. When she had finished, he smiled. "Charity, I'm not saying you assaulted your husband. Perhaps your story is true. I don't know because I wasn't there. What I can say, with decades of experience in such cases, is that if you tell your story to a jury, and Michael tells his side, the jury will believe him. Again," he continued, "I must advise you to consider a plea of guilty."

"But I didn't do it!" Charity replied. "Are you seriously telling me to admit to committing a crime I didn't do?"

Langdon sat back in his chair. "If you go to trial, there's a chance the DA will add other charges. Fourth degree assault is a misdemeanor. If they get a grand jury to indict you for aggravated assault, you're looking at a felony, and likely time in prison. If you plead guilty to the misdemeanor assault, there is no prison time and, you will likely be sentenced to a year or less of probation. Less time in court means lower legal fees. It may be a bitter pill, but it's your best option."

Charity's eyes drifted to the window where the world beyond moved in ignorance of her predicament. She wondered if there might be a sign out there—some divine whisper carried on the breeze—but the heavens remained silent, their azure expanse indifferent to her plight.

"Charity..." Langdon's voice brought her back. "What do you say?"

The papers lay before her, awaiting the mark of her pen. With a sigh of resignation, she signed her name.

"Thank you, Mrs. McBride," Langdon said. "I know that wasn't easy."

Easy.

The notion was a stranger to her current existence. Nothing about this journey was easy. Her path was paved with the stones of betrayal and lined with thorns of regret. But with the weight of her decision behind her, Charity felt the stirrings of something beyond resignation—an awareness that even when falsely accused, if she surrendered her pride, she could learn humility. Pride, after all, was the root of her troubles—at work and in relationships. She knew, though never admitted, that arrogance and self-centeredness destroyed her marriage. But here, in the attorney's office, she humbled herself and submitted to a cruel and indifferent process rather than screaming to be justified.

"Mrs. McBride," Langdon interjected, "there's another matter we need to address. As you know, your husband has filed for divorce. My expertise in family law is limited, but I can provide a general overview."

"I would be grateful for any advice." Charity said.

"Considering that you have no children and no significant assets to divide, the process should be relatively straightforward. If you'd like, I can represent you provided that your husband is willing to agree to a simple dissolution."

"Thank you," Charity replied, the words tasting of ash in her mouth. "Is there... could we try marriage counseling first?"

Langdon regarded her with eyes that had seen too many such pleas fall on barren ground. "I can only tell you what I know," he said. "Your husband made it quite clear that he is not interested in pursuing counseling. Unfortunately," he continued, "the path he's chosen seems inevitable.

Pain washed over Charity's face. She choked back a sob.

"Mrs. McBride, may I offer a personal perspective?"

"Sure."

Langdon leaned toward her. "It's tempting to think one might find closure or resolution in legal matters. But in reality, that seldom happens. Resolution, closure, and peace are only found outside the legal process, not within it."

His observation caught her off guard. Nevertheless, it rang true. "Thanks," Charity replied.

Langdon leaned back in his leather chair. "Charity," he said, pressing his fingertips together, "If I may advise, agreeing to the divorce would expedite the process. It's the most practical approach."

"But practicality doesn't always lead to the best decision," she said.

"Of course," he agreed, his tone acknowledging her struggle, "but consider the alternative—prolonged proceedings, additional costs, not to mention the emotional toll it will take. And, as I said, it seems divorce is inevitable."

"I can't give you an answer," Charity said, her voice subdued. She passed the signed documents across the desk. An unspoken prayer rose in her soul that somehow, she might avoid divorce.

33

The scent of lilac and sun-warmed earth met Charity as she stepped into the garden.

She hadn't come to work.

Or to explore.

Or even to heal.

She came to think.

To grieve.

The letter inside the envelope weighed like a stone in her coat pocket—the phrasing professional, detached.

Michael McBride has filed for dissolution of marriage...

She had expected anger. Or sorrow. But mostly, she felt like a failure.

Was she supposed to feel relief?

A soft rustling ahead drew her attention. The gardener was there, hunched beneath the trellis, pruning a long line of grapevines. His motions were slow, rhythmic. Deliberate.

"Hello," Charity said, her voice barely more than breath.

He looked up with a gentle smile. "You came at the right time."
"For what?"
"Clipping season."

She stepped closer. The vines were sprawling—green and unruly, some already bearing fruit. But others sagged with dead leaves and brittle stems.

The gardener reached for a dry cluster and snipped it free. It dropped to the soil.

"Not everything in a garden thrives," he said softly.

Charity's eyes drifted toward the dead branch. "Can't you save it?"

He shook his head. "This one stopped drawing from the root. Its vine grew hard. Its skin closed off. It no longer absorbed water."

She crouched beside him, her knees pressing into the warm soil. "So you cut it away."

"I released it."

She didn't respond. Her fingers found the envelope again, still hidden in her coat.

The gardener continued snipping, careful not to disturb the nearby fruit.

"There are vines," he said, "that drink deeply. That lean into the sun and open themselves to the wind. And there are others that close themselves off."

Charity nodded, tears gathering in her lashes. She did not speak again as they walked the rows together. The dead vine lay behind them, already fading into the soil.

34

The moon hung low over the garden. Its silver light filtered through the trees, casting long shadows across the path as Charity walked slowly, her coat wrapped tight around her. She had not spoken to Joshua all day. But she knew he would be here.

She found him by the stream, seated on a flat stone, his feet skimming the surface of the water. He didn't look up when she approached. Charity sat beside him and pulled the envelope from her pocket. "My attorney advised me to agree to a divorce. Michael won't consider counseling. Would I be quitting too soon?"

Joshua turned toward her. "What choice do you have?"

"But I promised," she whispered.

"You did," he agreed, "but not all covenants are kept by both parties. Didn't you say he had you arrested on false pretenses, and then obtained a restraining order? That doesn't leave you much choice."

"I keep thinking… if I were more patient. More forgiving. More obedient—maybe we'd still be together."

"You want to blame yourself," he replied, "but you could not go back to him now if you wanted. You would be arrested."

"How do I know it's the right decision?"

"There is no decision for you to make. Michael already made his choice. If you agree to it, you're acknowledging that the situation is beyond your control. But I want you to know this," he added, "I will be here for you, regardless."

35

Charity pulled her car into a municipal parking lot, found an open space, parked, and got out. Uri asked her to meet him at the festival. She had agreed, but skepticism nagged her. She sighed and walked across the street to the city park where the festival was in full swing.

As she approached, the sound of the crowd grew louder. Hesitantly, she passed through the gates. Bold swathes of fabric flapped above her head. The air was thick with the spicy tang of incense and the sizzle of exotic foods frying in open pans. Laughter mingled with the strum of guitars; the beat of drums reverberated against the soles of her feet.

She wove her way through the sea of seekers. Disbelief rested on her brow as she passed tents where crystals shimmered with promises of insight and tarot card readers whispered secrets of the future. Yet, beneath the cloak of skepticism, Charity's curiosity grew.

Suddenly, she smiled. Uri stood beneath a shade canopy. He

welcomed her, and asked her to have a seat.

Each greeting Uri offered to those who passed by seemed to acknowledge their hidden struggles. In a world of shamans and charlatans, Uri stood apart—as one who had traversed the valleys of his own soul, emerging not with gaudy tales of victory but with the quiet assurance of one who had faced the powers of darkness and defeated them.

A woman drew near, her spine curved into a question mark that seemed to weigh her down. With each step, her body spoke of a lifetime of silent endurance, of prayers for relief that never came. Charity watched as the woman approached Uri, the stranger's eyes alight with a fragile hope that illuminated her from within.

Uri greeted the woman. "Tell me your story," he said.

"I was diagnosed with scoliosis many years ago," she explained, "I've been to dozens of doctors and healers. I spent my life's savings, and no one has been able to help me."

"I understand," Uri said. "Let me see what I can do." His hands hovered above the woman's twisted back. "I command ligaments, muscles, tendons, bones, nerves, cartilage, and discs to be healed and strengthened in the name of Jesus. I command evil spirits to leave." Uri looked into the woman's eyes. "Move around," he said. "How do you feel?"

A look of astonishment spread across her face, her hand reaching to touch her own back to confirm the reality of what she felt. "There's no pain!" she exclaimed. Standing taller than when she had arrived, the woman whispered, "Thank you. How much do I owe you?"

"Nothing," Uri replied with a smile. "God loves you."

A wave of whispers washed over the onlookers who had witnessed the miracle. But Uri turned away, his attention shifting to the next person in need.

A man approached. He placed his hand on his head, squeezing his eyes shut against the stabbing pain that held him hostage. "Help me," he pleaded, his voice a hoarse whisper lost amid the festival noise.

Uri looked at the man and then closed his eyes. A smile spread across Uri's face. "Migraine?" he asked.

"Yes, how did you know?"

"Lucky guess," Uri said. "Let me help you." He held his hand near the man's forehead. "I command evil spirit to leave in the name of Jesus. Migraine, you are banished. Do not return."

The man's face relaxed, the creases in his forehead softening as if soothed by Uri's voice. The clench of his jaw eased. A sigh escaped his lips.

"How do you feel?" Uri asked.

"It's gone!" the man said in amazement.

Charity watched, her thoughts a mixture of awe and disbelief. The man's grateful nod as he departed testified to the quiet authority with which Uri operated.

Uri turned his attention to Charity. "What do you think?" he asked with a smile.

"How do you do it?" she asked, with a hint of suspicion.

"It's not as hard as it seems. I believe that people will be healed, and I act on that belief."

"Faith?" she asked incredulously.

"Bingo," he replied. "I think you should try it."

"I don't know how," she said in protest.

"I'll show you."

A woman watched them expectantly. Uri invited Charity to join him. Charity rose and stared at the woman, at a loss for how to proceed. Uri whispered in Charity's ear, and she nodded her head. "What can we help you with?" Charity asked nervously.

The woman pointed to her foot, which was encased in an orthopedic boot. "I have a torn Achille's tendon. My surgeon couldn't repair it."

Charity shot a look of concern at Uri. "Place your hand on her boot," Uri instructed. "Then command the tendon to be healed."

Charity placed her hand gently on the plastic boot, "I command this tendon to be healed. I command it to be reattached in the name of Jesus." Charity looked at Uri. "Now what?"

"Ma'am," Uri said, "Can you tell me how your foot feels?"

The woman felt her foot. "It doesn't feel any different."

Discouraged, Charity turned to walk away. Uri looked at the woman, "Stay right here. I'll be back in a minute."

Uri followed Charity. "Where are you going?"

"This isn't working. I feel like a fool."

"I should have warned you," Uri said, "You're a beginner. It doesn't always work the first time. I felt like a fool praying for people who weren't healed when I first started. But I kept going. If you quit now, you'll never know what could have been. Let's go back and try again."

Charity sighed. "Okay." She returned to where the woman was and placed her hand on the plastic boot. "I command this tendon to be healed... right now.

Uri looked at the woman. "How does it feel?"

She shifted her weight and surprise spread across her face. "Wait a minute," she said. "Can I borrow a chair?" Uri placed his chair in front of her. She sat down, removed the Velcro straps from the boot, and then slipped it off. The woman stood up and walked back and forth in front of them. "Are you kidding me?" she said. "Wow. It feels normal!" A low rumble spread through the crowd behind her.

"How did you... how did I...?"

"Give us a few minutes, folks," Uri said to the crowd. "I'm training a student and we need a moment. We'll be with you all shortly."

Uri motioned to a chair and sat down beside Charity. "I know you're wondering how this is possible. So let me explain. You know how in the gospels Jesus and the disciples healed the sick and cast out demons?"

"I recall reading about that," Charity said.

"God has given us the same power and authority they used. We can do the things they did."

"Wait," Charity interrupted. "I was taught to ask God to heal people."

"So was I," Uri replied, "but I haven't seen anyone healed that way, have you?"

"No," she confessed.

"You have the Spirit of God living inside of you," he continued.

"Correct," she said, nodding.

"The power that created the universe resides in you. So, all you need to do is release it. You've used a defibrillator, haven't you?"

"Of course," she replied.

"A defibrillator releases energy, right?"

"Yes."

"And it brings the dead back to life."

Charity's mouth hung open as the meaning of his analogy became clear.

"So…" she began, "all I need to do is release the electricity… I mean, the power inside of me to help people get healed?"

"Exactly," Uri said.

"But how?"

"Faith," he said, allowing the word to sink into her consciousness. "Belief. Assurance. Confidence. Whatever you choose to call it. When I see someone who needs healing, I tell myself they will be healed. It builds confidence. It creates assurance. That's what releases the power of God. Power does the healing. Faith is the trigger."

Charity suddenly stood up. "I get it," she said. "I totally get it." She looked at the crowd. A child caught her attention. She motioned for the young girl to approach. Charity saw no obvious sign of illness or injury. "Hey, sweetie," she said. "My name is Charity, what's yours?"

The girl looked at her mother. "Her name is Jasmine," the woman replied. "I was wondering..." she hesitated, "if you could pray for her vision. She's nearly blind in her left eye."

Charity glanced at Uri nervously.

"You got this," he said.

She turned to the girl. Closing her eyes, Charity breathed deeply, her own skepticism melting away with each inhalation. She placed her hands near the girl's eyes. A warmth emanated from her palms, a force she had never known before—a gentle surge of power that was tangible. In her mind, she saw herself releasing a flow of power into the girl's eyes. The bright colors and festive songs around them faded into nothingness as the connection between healer and hopeful was established. With each breath, Charity's trepidation drained, replaced by a confidence that flowed from her soul to her fingers. "I command your eyes to be healed."

Uri bent toward Jasmine. "Do you feel anything?" he asked.

She shook her head excitedly. "It feels warm."

"All right, kiddo, I think we should test your vision." Her mother excitedly knelt before the girl and told Jasmine to close her right eye and say how many fingers she was holding up.

"Three!" the girl shouted with glee. "Mommy, I can see!"

Jasmine's mother gave Charity a long embrace. "Thank you, so much," she said. "Thank you for being the hands of God." Tears welled up in Charity's eyes. The woman took Jasmine's hand, and they left, giving Charity and Uri a final wave.

"Way to go," Uri said to Charity. He raised his hand. She slapped it.

"I can't believe this is happening."

Into the afternoon, Charity found herself amid a sea of souls, each one a vessel of hidden pain and unspoken dreams. There was the elderly man with hands gnarled by arthritis, his fingers unfolding like petals at dawn. She touched a boy with eczema and watched the redness vanish. With each encounter, Charity's confidence grew.

As dusk settled over the festival, painting the sky in amber and rose, she retreated to the quiet of a nearby bench. The day's events replayed in her mind. She had stepped into the river of the unknown, only to find herself carried along on the currents by faith and love.

Charity looked up at the first evening star twinkling in the darkening sky. A profound peace settled over her as if the celestial light whispered assurances that she was exactly where she needed to be. Uri saw her sitting alone and took a seat beside her.

"That was quite a day," he said.

She shot him a look of gratitude. "It was amazing."

"Charity, why did you become a paramedic?"

She thought for a moment. "Because I want to help people."

"How many people did you heal working on the ambulance?"

"None," she said remorsefully.

"How many people did you see healed today?"

"I lost count," she said, smiling.

"Not bad for a rookie."

At that moment, Charity realized this was more than merely an apprenticeship. It was a gateway—the entrance into a realm where skepticism gave way to faith—where the physical encountered the divine. Taking a breath that tasted like the first drop of rain on parched earth, she rested, convinced that the journey leading to her destiny had finally begun.

36

Charity sat beside Uri on a weathered park bench. Laughter bubbled from a nearby group of children chasing pigeons under a cerulean sky near the center of the city.

"Let's do an exercise," Uri's said.

"I ran three miles this morning, I'm good," Charity said sarcastically.

"That's hilarious," Uri replied.

"Thanks for humoring me."

"Okay, miss smarty pants, this will be a spiritual exercise."

"Why didn't you say so?" she asked.

Uri gave Charity a friendly shove. "Can we begin?"

"You're the teacher."

"All right, I want you to close your eyes and block out from your memory anything that's visible in the physical world. Focus your mind on what you see in the spiritual dimension."

Charity closed her eyes and consciously blocked out buildings, trees, and people that remained in her field of view.

"Look for shadows or anything that seems extremely dark or objects that seem unusually bright," Uri said.

"I'm looking."

"You'll eventually see something. But your nature will be to think you're imagining it. You have to learn to trust what you see."

"I see something." Charity opened her eyes to check what was present in the physical world.

"What is it?"

Charity pointed to a woman who was walking toward them. "Do you see that woman?" she asked.

"Yes," Uri replied.

Charity closed her eyes. "She has something black hanging onto her, like a massive leech."

"What do you think it is?"

"A demon?" she asked.

"Bingo."

Charity smiled. "That is cool as hell."

"It's just the beginning."

"There's more?"

He chuckled. "A lot more. Close your eyes again and tell me what else you see."

Charity closed her eyes and blocked out physical objects from her mind. "Oh, crap…" she said, "this is no bueno."

Uri smiled. "What do you see?"

"Lots and lots of those frickin' demons. That guy has one on his back," she said, pointing to a man walking with a child. "That lady has two of them around her head. Please tell me I'm imagining this."

"We regret to inform you that you are not hallucinating and this is not a drill," Uri replied. "They're as real as you and me."

"Now, look toward the fountain."

Charity looked at a fountain near the center of the park and closed her eyes. In the dark, she saw the glow of an imposing figure—an angel of light. Its massive wings were unfurled, its feathers shimmering like liquid silver. In its hand, it held a sword.

"An angel…" Charity said, awestruck by the sight.

"They're all around us."

She watched the angel, its countenance intimidating but assuring.

"Can it see us?" she wondered aloud.

"It's worse," Uri said. "It can hear us."

"Are you serious?"

"There's only one way to find out," he replied. "You could give him a command."

"What?" Charity asked incredulously. "Are you crazy? What would I tell an angel to do?"

Uri pointed to a homeless man asleep on the grass. "Do you see that man over there?"

Charity looked at the man. "Yes."

"Close your eyes and tell me what you see in the spirit."

Charity closed her eyes. "Oh, crap!" she gasped.

"What do you see?"

"There's a demon sitting on his head. It has talons. They're buried into his skull. I think it's talking to him."

"That's what I see. Now, command the angel to free the man sleeping on the ground."

She hesitated as the enormity of wielding such authority intimidated her. But she thought of her own afflictions and how grateful she was for the help she had received from Joshua and the gardener.

Charity closed her eyes and focused on the angel by the fountain. "Angel of light," she began, "free that homeless man from the demon that is tormenting him."

The angel responded immediately. Its wings unfurled like sails catching the wind, and it moved toward the sleeping man. Charity watched intently with her eyes closed. The demon recoiled at the approach of the angel. As it neared the man, the angel paused as if waiting for another command. Indignation rose in Charity's soul at the sight of the demon preying on the helpless man.

"Incinerate that evil demon," she commanded.

The angel raised its huge sword, which had transformed into a fiery blade. It lowered the sword with a swift motion, striking the demon. It writhed and hissed as flames seared through its body. Those nearby took no notice of the battle unfolding in their midst, blind to the spiritual war they could not perceive. Smoke billowed where the demon once was, tendrils of darkness evaporating into nothingness.

Charity exhaled slowly. "Wow. That was insane!"

"Well done."

"Uri," Charity said, "I feel as though I've been asleep, dreaming… existing in a fake world. But now, for the first time, I see."

"It's a jarring awakening, isn't it? And as bizarre as it might sound, what you've seen is just a glimpse. There's a vast spiritual world around us, with all sorts of beings doing crazy things you've never imagined."

"Is this my destiny then?" Charity asked. "Am I called to be a soldier in this war?"

"What do you think?"

"After all these years, I think I may have finally found my calling. But I need help. Do you know any gurus who might take me under their wing and show me the ropes?" she asked sarcastically.

"I'll ask around."

37

The garden waited. Its silence was not empty—it pulsed with memory, with longing, with echoes of names whispered long ago and never forgotten. The air was thick with dew, and the scent of turned soil mingled with lavender and ash. Here, time did not pass; it breathed.

The gardener knelt beside a small bed of marigolds. Some had bloomed; others had withered. He did not rush the work. He moved gently, brushing aside dead leaves, nudging roots with calloused fingers, as if coaxing them back to life. The soil was not resistant—it was weary. Hardened in places, cracked in others. He knew it well.

Above him, branches arched like cathedral vaults, sunlight trickling through in slanted beams. A gate stood at the far end of the garden, still open, though she had not entered in many days.

He stood and surveyed the rows of memory, his robes dusted with pollen and shadow. Each path led to a piece of her—buried, protected, forgotten. Some sections teemed with wildflowers.

Others lay fallow, choked with vine and thorn. But all of it was hers. And he tended it as if it were his own.

A rustle drew his gaze to a grove of hollow trees. A young girl peeked out, clutching a worn scrap of blanket. She did not run when he looked at her. That, too, was progress.

He smiled softly. "You're safe here," he said. His voice didn't echo—it settled, like mist. "She's coming back soon."

The child nodded once, then withdrew into her hollow. He did not follow. Healing was not a harvest to be forced—it was the fruit of patience.

The old man moved deeper into the garden, stopping before a featureless bed he had left untouched. In years past, the soil had been rich, but now, it was as hard as a stone, sealed shut by shame and silence. This was the place of deepest sorrow. He knelt slowly, pressing a trowel to the ground. He tapped it with the heel of his hand. At last, the earth gave way. He moved the trowel and tapped it again. He moved it a third time and struck it with his hand.

He closed his eyes.

A breeze stirred.

Something shifted in the spirit.

She was dreaming again.

38

Nestled in her tent, Charity drifted off to sleep. Minutes later, hovering between waking and deep rest, she stood in a narrow hallway carved from alabaster. A rhythmic banging—measured and deliberate—echoed through the corridor.

As she turned a corner, the sound intensified, reverberating from behind a heavy wooden door to her right. The door was dark and ancient, its surface scarred by time. Charity reached for the massive bronze handle. It opened without a sound.

Beyond lay a radiant courtroom, glowing with heavenly opulence. Marble pillars reached toward a ceiling fashioned of hammered gold. The light shimmered with a purity she could feel on her skin.

Charity stepped forward cautiously as if entering a burning building. Amid the ethereal beauty, her eyes were drawn to the judge seated on the bench—an older man who bore an uncanny resemblance to the gardener.

To her right stood a dark silhouette whose shape and presence defied classification. Zolgreth. The demon's twisted form carved a grotesque outline against the celestial glow. He turned and hissed, "She's not supposed to be here!"

Charity looked to her left and recognized a familiar face. Approaching the defense table, she pulled out a chair and sat beside the blue-eyed man.

"Your timing is impeccable," Joshua said with a warm smile. "We're just about to begin."

Charity turned to him, her eyes brimming with a hundred unspoken questions.

The courtroom fell silent. The judge struck the gavel.

"Let the accuser state the accusation," he declared.

Zolgreth stepped forward. "Charity McBride," he began, "is guilty of pride, envy, and wrath." Charity's cheeks flushed with anger. "Deceit," he continued. "Lust. A gluttony for attention and approval. By the testimony of her husband, she has stolen property, committed adultery, and used illegal drugs."

Charity rose in protest. "That... that evil thing is lying!"

"Charity."

Joshua's single word cut through the noise. She froze, then slowly sank back into her seat.

"This isn't fair," she whispered. "I've done nothing wrong."

"Charity," Joshua interrupted gently. "Have you considered your sins?"

The question shattered her defenses. Her shoulders slumped. Shame washed over her as hidden memories surfaced—sins she had never spoken aloud.

"Is that what this is about?" she asked quietly. "Am I on trial for every sin I've ever committed?"

"Yes."

She met his gaze and saw no judgment—only mercy.

"I'm not perfect," she said, offering one last argument.

"You're not," Joshua agreed. "And your accuser knows it. Everyone who stands before this court is guilty of something."

"Then what's the point?"

"This court," he said, "is unlike any you've known. Here, the only plea is guilty."

Her voice trembled. "How can a guilty plea save me?"

"Because I'm not just your attorney. I am your defense."

She blinked. "I don't understand."

"When I was crucified, my blood took the punishment for your sins."

Tears welled in her eyes. The significance of his sacrifice, which had always been an abstract concept in her mind, now settled over her, overwhelming and tender.

"But… what can I do?" she asked.

"With your permission, I will represent you. My legal strategy is simple: I will plead my own blood on your behalf."

The brilliance of the plan filled her heart with sudden warmth. She smiled. "Do you think it'll work?"

He winked. "It's worth a shot. And as my bride, you're entitled to my best defense."

Charity gazed into his fiery eyes. He leaned in and embraced her, firm and tender.

"I love you," he whispered.

"I love you too," she said, choking back tears. After composing herself, she turned to Zolgreth, then to the judge, and finally back to Joshua. "Let's do this."

Joshua rose. "Your Honor," he said, "I stand to advocate for Charity McBride. I will represent her in this matter."

"How does the defendant plead?" the judge asked.

"Your Honor," Joshua replied, "I enter a plea of guilty on

behalf of my bride. As the plaintiff correctly noted, her sins are many—like all humankind. But this is why I came. I walked among them, suffered at their hands, and let my blood be spilled. That blood now pleads on her behalf."

The judge nodded solemnly, then struck his gavel.

"Charity McBride," he pronounced, "you stand before this court accused. You do not deny the accusation. Yet, in light of the defense presented, I declare you innocent."

Zolgreth recoiled. "No!" he shrieked. "This is a miscarriage of justice! She's guilty—she *admitted* it! She belongs to us!"

But his cries found no audience. The judge banged the gavel.

"Angels, escort the plaintiff out of the courtroom."

Four angels descended. Their touch was firm but gentle as they led the snarling demon away, his shrieks fading into the distance.

Charity turned to Joshua and reached for his hands.

"Thank you," she whispered.

Then, without another word, she walked to the back of the courtroom, placed her hand on the door, pushed it open, and stepped into the hallway.

She awoke.

39

Zolgreth's shadow moved like a deranged marionette against the walls of the alley. "Useless," he muttered under his breath, "All useless," he repeated, voicing frustration over his failed attempts to break Charity's spirit. In his mind's eye lingered the image of his victim, a flawed and imperfect woman who proved nevertheless to be resilient in the face of his most insidious attacks.

From the depths of the alley, Valdor emerged. The flickering glow of a streetlamp chose that moment to flare, casting a brief yet intense illumination upon the senior demon. "Charity yet stands," Valdor said, his voice weaving through the alley with the ease of a serpent slithering through the grass. Valdor's stride was slow and deliberate, the echo of his steps a metronome counting each of Zolgreth's failures. "Zolgreth!" Valdor shouted, "You know that we are never to be seen by humans under any circumstances."

Zolgreth flinched at the rebuke. "Master, I beg your forbearance," he stammered. "Charity was not supposed to be in court. Someone told her to be there."

"Excuses?" Valdor replied. "Is that the best you can do?"

Zolgreth's eyes, dull and fearful, darted away, unable to meet the gaze of his mentor. His mind reeled with the implications of his inadequacy.

Valdor's shadow stretched across the narrow alley like a dark prophecy. "Zolgreth, you fail to grasp the gravity of the situation," the senior demon said. "Should Charity awaken to our plans, should she see the intent of our labor, it would be catastrophic."

Zolgreth listened in silence.

"Imagine," Valdor continued, "the forces that would rally behind her, the healing that would restore all that we have labored to break. The chaos that would erupt in the heavens, tipping scales that have long favored our dominion. Our kind, banished to the dry places for eternity." His gaze found the hunched figure of Zolgreth, pinning him with its intensity. "Is that the legacy you intend to leave?"

Zolgreth determined he would not be the reason for their undoing. "I will not falter," he vowed.

"Do you intend to weary me with empty promises, Zolgreth?"

"No, Master."

"Now that Charity has seen you," Valdor said, "a change of strategy is in order. You cannot allow her to sense your presence again. You must become the whisper in the wind, seen by none, felt by all."

Zolgreth listened, his fear giving way to the promise of deceit yet to be mastered.

"Stealth," Valdor continued, "is the art we perfect, deception the brush we wield. You must learn to paint despair not with broad strokes but with the subtlest of touches." His hand swept across the dim landscape, casting angular shapes upon the walls.

"Behold," Valdor pointed toward the darkness where vermin

scurried, "even the rat knows its power lies within the unseen crevices of this world."

Zolgreth absorbed his master's words.

"Consider the stray dog that rummages through the refuse, the crow that watches from the wire, they can be vessels for our cause. Tools to fray the edges of her sanity. Charity is but one thread in the tapestry of this war, and she must be broken."

The sermon brought a flicker of inspiration to Zolgreth's eyes, a spark amid the dampened embers of mind. Valdor imparted more than instruction; he offered a lifeline to a drowning minion.

"Use the unwitting, the ignored, the discarded. Let humanity's own neglect be the conduit for our influence."

And there, in the heart of the alley, where light dared not linger, Zolgreth felt the stirrings of a plan. It was embryonic, fragile, but it was there—a path forward, woven from Valdor's counsel—a way to remain shrouded yet present in the life of the one they sought to destroy. Zolgreth nodded. "Yes, Master. I shall become the unseen whisper. Charity will not be safe even in her own mind."

"Your zeal is noted," Valdor said dryly, "but let it be tempered with caution. Our work has consequences. Fail again, and you will regret it for eternity." With those final words, Zolgreth watched Valdor's silhouette dissolve into the darkness.

The threat settled upon Zolgreth like a mantle weighted with the gravity of his unholy quest, the air filled with ultimatums, the silence punctuated only by a distant siren. Despite the threat, Zolgreth's confidence arose as he entertained possibilities. Disguises, he mused, must be as numerous as the stars, each one a mask to conceal his presence. He would not be defeated by these humans. He would weave a web so diabolical not even the blue-eyed man could untangle it.

40

Charity walked beside Joshua through the garden to a destination unknown to her. Joshua carried an ornate staff, which, when they stopped, he would lean on.

"I had a dream where I met a young woman in a suit of armor." Charity said. "I felt like I knew her, but she refused to trust me."

They walked in silence between rows of flowers, and Charity spoke. "I think I need to find her. Will you help me?"

Joshua smiled. "I thought you'd never ask."

He led her away from the tended flowerbeds. The path passed beneath the massive arch, and they entered a wooded area. Joshua turned and followed a barely visible trail. The terrain became uneven, with roots sprawling across their path. Joshua used the staff to maintain his balance.

A hush fell over the woods, the only sound the crunch of leaves and the occasional call of a distant bird.

As they walked, Charity felt a gentle pull in her soul, drawing her onward. They continued in silence, the path dipping into a ravine. On the far side of the ravine, patches of dappled light appeared before them, and finally, they emerged from the woods into a clearing. Before them loomed a two-story stone house, its exterior steeped in shades of gray. The structure was fortress-like, imposing in its silence, with thick stone walls on all sides, crowned with coils of razor wire.

Warning signs were posted throughout the yard. Their words—*No Trespassing, Beware, Private Property*—served not only as cautions but as declarations, guarding the secrets within from prying eyes.

Charity's attention was drawn to movement in an open window on the second story. There, framed by curtains, stood a young woman. Her posture was rigid, her silhouette vigilant as she watched Charity and Joshua approach. She assessed their intentions, her gaze darting between them. Charity knew well the ways of silent interrogation—the doubt and caution that come from one who has known betrayal and wears its scars like armor.

Joshua's hand lightly touched Charity's shoulder. "Speak to her," he whispered, "you must gain her trust."

Charity knew the girl in the window from her dream. She was encased in layers of self-preservation woven from threads of past deceptions. To unravel such defenses required more than words—it demanded proof that one could be trusted.

"Hello!" Charity called to her.

The young woman's expression remained unchanged, yet her eyes flickered with a hint of curiosity. She leaned forward, the barest inch, a silent concession to the voice reaching out to her.

"I know you might not believe me," Charity continued, each word carefully chosen, "but we've come here because we care—because I care."

The young woman spoke. "Why should I trust you? Everyone says that before they stab you in the back."

Charity stepped closer. "I've been betrayed by those I trusted. I understand the deception that lurks behind promises."

"Easy for you to say," the young woman retorted, but now her words were laced with a tremor, a small crack in her defensive wall. "You're out there, free. While I'm stuck here, guarding against lies and deceit. You don't know what it's like."

"Maybe not," Charity admitted, allowing her own vulnerability to surface. "But pain recognizes pain. And healing is a path we can walk together."

A pause followed, heavy with consideration. The young woman's eyes searched Charity's, sifting through the sincerity of her plea, weighing the risks of lowering her guard against the possibility of finding peace.

"Prove it," came the challenge, a whisper of hope disguised as skepticism. "Show me that you're different."

Charity met her gaze unflinchingly, the glow of determination kindling within her. She had committed to the journey of mending fractures, no matter how arduous the road. In seeking trust from the tormented fragments of her soul, she learned to set aside her mistrust. And in offering healing, she bet everything on the slim chance that she might become whole again.

Charity stepped closer to the fence. In closing the physical gap, she sought to bridge the emotional chasm between them. "Do you remember me?" Charity asked.

The woman in the window peered down, her guarded expression softening momentarily as recognition flickered like a shooting star streaking across the night sky.

"Yes," she confessed, the word barely escaping the confines of her lips. "I know you."

Joshua stepped beside Charity. "Ask her what it is that she guards against."

Charity nodded. "What is it that you protect so fiercely?"

"I'm the keeper," she said, her tone infused with self-imposed duty. "The one who stands watch, who shields you from those who would exploit your trust."

Charity listened, her mind replaying battles with those who had betrayed her. "My protector," she whispered as recognition spread across her face. She took a step back from the wall. "I'm grateful for all you have done for me, but I'm no longer a fractured woman in need of guarding. The time has come for me to be my own guardian. And when I fail," she continued, gazing at Joshua, "I have a protector more powerful than you."

A gust of wind whispered through the trees as if to affirm her words, yet the young woman remained steadfast. "Your conviction is noble," the woman responded, "but our memory tells another story. Charity often made foolish pacts with people she swore we could trust—are we to ignore all of this?"

Charity ached as scenes raced through her mind, recalling each betrayal. Her father's broken promise on her birthday. Her best friend embarrassing her in front of the class. She swore an oath they would never do it again. And now, she was speaking with the enforcer.

Joshua stepped forward. "Allow me to be your guardian," he said to the woman in the window. "Under my watch, no evil will cause you harm."

"Why should we trust you?" the woman asked.

"How can I prove that I am worthy of your trust?"

The young woman met his gaze. "The forest is filled with dark spirits. They mock and torment us night and day. If what you claim is true, it should be easy for you to defeat them."

Watching their discourse, Charity felt the interplay of fear and faith within herself. She sensed the young woman's conflict—the prospect of being released from an endless vigil was both tempting and terrifying.

Joshua stepped toward the wall. "Show us where these dark spirits are."

The young woman hesitated, her eyes flickering with the ghost of old torments. But in the silence, beneath the watchful boughs of ancient trees, a spark of hope alighted in her soul. With a slow nod, she descended from her place at the window—a sentinel abandoning her post for the first time in ages.

They ventured together into the woods, where the light was dim. "Here," the young woman said. "This is where they linger." Her arm, outstretched, trembling as though pointing would summon the evil she sought to keep at bay.

Joshua stepped forward, his staff held before him. The ancient and gnarled wood illuminated with a power that pulsed against the creeping darkness. Then, as if the heavens had lent their light, the tip of his staff ignited with a brilliance that cut through the shadows.

"Be gone," he said, thrusting the staff forward as it released a pulse of energy that tore through the fabric of the forest.

A dark spirit recoiled as the light struck it. It wailed before disintegrating into wisps of vapor.

The young woman's eyes widened. Fear mingled with wonder, and the veil of her skepticism lifted. "By what power…?" she whispered, her voice trailing off as she searched Joshua's face for answers.

"Love," he replied, suggesting that love was indeed the greatest force—capable of vanquishing the deepest darkness.

"Over there," she uttered, pointing toward a shadow that

slithered across the ground. Joshua turned to face the adversary. As before, the staff responded to his command, firing a bolt of celestial light into the woods. The demon writhed before dissipating into the ether.

The young woman gasped and turned to Joshua. Her skepticism, once as hard as the stone walls of her home, crumbled by the undeniable evidence of Joshua's power.

"Will you let me guard Charity's soul?" Joshua asked.

She hesitated, a vestige of her stubbornly resisting the possibility of placing her trust in another. But the battle she had just witnessed—the collision of light against dark—had proven that he was a better protector.

"Yes," she said at last, "I will let you."

It was a declaration of surrender but also of hope, a turning point where the possibility of healing loomed larger than the specter of her fears. She looked at Charity, truly looked, and saw not someone to shield but a reflection of herself.

Joshua reached out, his hand glowing under the dimness of the forest. The young woman gazed at the offered palm, pondering the immensity of her surrender.

The woman's arms were marred with scars. "Let me heal you," he said softly.

She nodded as she placed her trembling hand in his. The touch was light, but the power was monumental—a river breaking through a dam long overdue for demolition.

As Joshua's warmth enveloped her wounds, both seen and unseen, the young woman's eyes fluttered closed. Her features, etched with years of vigilance and scars of battles past, relaxed. The healing energy pulsed around them; golden threads wove through the fabric of her being, stitching together torn edges of soul and spirit.

Charity watched, her own heart swelling with a mix of awe and anticipation.

After her healing was complete, Joshua addressed the young woman. "Are you ready to become one with Charity?"

"Will I cease to exist?" she asked.

"No," Joshua said with a smile. "You were once an integrated part of Charity. And then, due to trauma, you were separated. When you are integrated, it will be as it was before. You will always be a valuable part of her."

She smiled. "I'm ready."

"Hold each other's hands," Joshua said. "Close your eyes and envision your hearts beating as one. The two clasped hands and closed their eyes. "Accept the other's pain as yours. Tell the other you love them and forgive them."

Charity spoke first. "Thank you for protecting me," she said. "I love you and I forgive for any mistakes you've made."

"I love you, Charity," the young woman replied. "It has been an honor protecting you. I forgive you, and more than anything, I want peace." The young woman's body flickered with light and then disappeared. At last, Charity opened her eyes. They were no longer two souls fractured by life's cruelty but one—healed and whole.

Beneath the watchful gaze of the heavens, amid a grove that whispered of eternal secrets, Charity found herself no longer a mosaic of jagged pieces but a seamless portrait of resilience and hope.

41

Charity awoke to a chill. She lay still for a moment, nestled in her sleeping bag, allowing the webs of dreams to release their hold. Finally, with a gentle stretch, she greeted the day.

As her thoughts wandered, weaving memories of yesterday's victories, she unzipped the tent and stepped outside.

Without warning, a vicious snarl shattered the silence. Charity glanced to her left and saw a large dog running toward her, barking viciously. There was no time for thought; she instinctively retreated backward as the canine launched itself at her with startling speed.

The dog bore down upon her, its claws ripping at her skin, its mouth straining to bite her face. With hands outstretched, she met the beast head-on, wrestling to control its jaws that sought to rip her apart. Her palms pressed against the fur of its snout, her fingers working to muzzle the onslaught of teeth. Claws like daggers raked at her, tearing through her clothing and skin.

Suddenly, Charity's vision blurred and then became crystal

clear. In a trance, she saw not only the dog but a demon that controlled it by force. In the vision, Zolgreth emerged as a puppeteer, his fingers twisted around strings that ensnared the dog's soul. The demon commanded the scene—the dog, his unwitting victim, thrashed under an invisible yoke, obeying his every command.

Charity's attention was drawn to another scene that played out before her eyes. She saw a blazing fireball resting in the sling of a massive catapult. Feeling her strength slipping away, she uttered a desperate plea. "God Almighty, destroy this demon. Let the fire of the heaven consume this evil creature."

She watched as the orb of fire rocketed through the heavens arcing and then returning to earth—a celestial inferno cascading from the sky. The fire landed on its mark, enveloping Zolgreth and leaving him writhing as it seared through the threads of control he had spun. The flames roared to devour the demon, yet they moved around the dog with an ethereal gentleness.

The dog, now released from the demon's control, staggered back with a whimper. Its eyes, once filled with ferocity, softened into a confused haze as it scampered away.

Charity lay on the ground her heart pounding in her chest. With trembling fingers, she wiped at her cheek, her hand coming away wet and warm with blood. A sharp sting radiated from where the dog's claws had punctured her flesh.

She crawled into the tent and reached into her backpack, fumbling for the gauze bandages. She inspected her body and applied bandages to the largest lacerations.

Pushing through the tent flap, Charity emerged to find Joshua and the gardener approaching. Holding a wad of gauze to her cheek, she managed a weak yet wry smile. "I always wondered if mornings in Eden came with a side of canine chaos," she quipped.

"Even paradise knew trouble," Joshua replied. "But it's the trials that help us grow."

She chuckled softly. "Well, I'd prefer my growth opportunities with fewer teeth, if you don't mind."

He smiled at her, the warmth in his eyes melting away the remnants of fear. "Your spirit is unbroken."

"Unbroken, maybe, but definitely bent," she said, gingerly touching the bandage on her face. Charity glanced at the gardener, who gave an encouraging nod.

Joshua moved toward the center of the garden, gathering twigs and branches scattered about, and arranging them. The old man joined him, adding larger pieces of wood to the pile. Charity watched them in silence.

Joshua reached into a satchel lying on the ground and produced a loaf of bread and a small pot, which he placed near the fire. "Nothing heals the soul like breaking bread with friends," he added, beginning to prepare a simple meal.

Charity lowered herself to the ground, watching Joshua move with an effortless elegance. "Thank you. I came here without much money." She glanced at the gardener. "I thought by now, the little cash I had would be gone. But your kindness has provided everything I've needed. And I still have most of my cash."

As they ate, the sun broke through a bank of clouds above the horizon, its rays painting the sky with streaks of orange and pink. As her body relaxed against the earth's gentle embrace, Charity allowed her gaze to drift across the garden. The chaos that had erupted a moment ago seemed distant now. As she watched Joshua tend the fire, its flames cast a warm glow that kissed her skin and mended the chill of her earlier ordeal.

42

Steam from the espresso machine curled into the air, merging with the murmur of the coffee shop. Charity stood behind the counter, her fingers moving across the register keys, taking orders during the morning rush.

"Large cappuccino, please," a customer requested, breaking through the din of conversation.

"Coming right up," Charity replied.

The bell above the door announced another arrival at the coffee shop. Uri paused just inside the door, surprised to see Charity behind the counter. He gave her a silent wave as he stepped toward the counter.

Charity smiled. "Good morning, Uri. How's the world treating you today?"

He leaned against the counter. "Can't complain."

Charity reached for a clean cup, poured a dab of cream, and then filled it with black coffee. Uri watched, captivated by the confidence she displayed in a new environment.

"Here you go." Charity slid the cup across the counter. Uri handed her his card. She swiped it and handed it back.

"Thank you," he said, his fingers closing around the mug.

As the morning conversations filled the coffee shop, Charity noticed a new patron—a woman in a wheelchair approaching the counter.

"Good morning," Charity said, "What can I start for you?"

The woman looked up, the lines of fatigue on her face softening. "Just a small coffee, black, please."

As Charity nodded, she couldn't help but notice the subtle tension that seemed to hold the woman's shoulders captive. "Would it be all right if I prayed for you?" she asked.

The woman paused. A glimmer of hope flickered to life in her eyes, mingling with the skepticism born of countless disappointments. "Of course," the woman finally said.

Charity glanced over her shoulder at the sound of frothing milk. She saw her colleague, a young man helping with the morning rush, and caught his attention with a motion of her hand.

"Could you take over for a moment?" Charity asked.

The young man followed Charity's gaze to the woman in the wheelchair. "She needs a small black coffee… on me."

He nodded and prepared her drink.

Charity entered the lobby and stood beside the woman in the wheelchair. She placed her hand gently on the woman's shoulder.

"Lord," Charity said, "you are the God who restores and heals the broken-hearted. I ask you now to touch this precious woman. I command her body to be healed. I command broken joints to be mended and pain to be released. I command spirits of infirmity to leave."

At that moment, a hush fell over the coffee shop. Patrons paused to acknowledge the rarity of what they were witnessing.

"May healing flow like a river, may it rise like the dawn after the longest night," she concluded.

"Thank you," whispered the woman in the wheelchair.

"Try to stand," Charity said.

With a look of determination, she grasped the arms of the wheelchair. Her body, a dormant silhouette for over a decade, responded to an invisible call. Muscles long resigned to stillness, summoned their forgotten strength. And then, she rose.

"I… I'm standing!" she gasped, the declaration echoing through the shop, which had become silent.

Uri watched as the woman took her first step. A murmur erupted from the shop's patrons. Uri took the woman's hand. "You're doing great," he said, "keep going." She walked to the shop's front door and back, beaming with joy at every step. The young man behind the counter handed Charity a cup of black coffee, and Charity gave it to the woman, who carried it to a table where she took a seat.

"Thank you, my child," the woman said.

Charity turned to Uriel. "What do we do with the wheelchair?" she asked.

"If she doesn't need it anymore, she can always donate it," he said, smiling.

43

Three months later

The café was closed, the espresso machine scrubbed, the chairs stacked on the tables. Charity untied her apron and slipped out the back door into the warm night. It had been a long shift, but she wasn't ready to go home. Her stomach growled.

She walked two blocks to the bistro-pub at the corner. It was a Friday night hot spot—exposed brick walls, string lights, laughter spilling out through open windows. The scent of grilled steak and rosemary drifted into the street.

She slipped inside, found a table near the back, and ordered a glass of wine and a ribeye.

She was halfway through her salad when she looked up—and saw him.

Travis.

He stood near the host stand, scanning the room, looking for a seat. His hair was longer. He'd grown a beard. But the posture was unmistakable—strong, a little guarded. Familiar.

Their eyes met.

He paused. Then nodded once.

She hesitated… then raised her hand slowly and motioned toward the empty chair across from her.

He approached cautiously. "You sure?" he asked, half-smiling.

Charity nodded. "Only if you don't mind being interrogated over dinner."

Travis chuckled nervously and took a seat.

They shared small talk. He had a new partner. A rookie paramedic that needed coaching. Charity told him she'd traded adrenaline for almond milk and espresso.

"You look good," he said eventually. "Lighter."

"Thanks. You look… hairy," she said with a laugh.

Travis rubbed his beard. "I'm not sure if the new look agrees with me."

There was an awkward pause in the conversation.

Travis traced the rim of his water glass. "I wasn't sure you'd want to talk to me again."

"I wasn't sure either," Charity said. "Back then, I thought you were wrong. About me, I mean. You called me out. Criticized my decisions. I hated you for it." She looked around the room and then swallowed hard. "But now… I see you were right. About everything."

Travis sat speechless for a moment. Finally, he leaned in. "There's something you should know."

His tone shifted. More serious.

"Two weeks ago, Lieutenant Myers was found passed out on the floor of the medic office. He had a needle in his arm and an empty vial beside him."

Charity blinked. "What?"

"He overdosed. He lived. The chief personally escorted him to a treatment facility."

Charity stared at him, stunned.

Travis continued. "Turns out, he'd been stealing the narcotics for months. Maybe longer. He covered his tracks like a pro. Paperwork was always perfect. And no one—*no one*—suspected him."

"Charlie Myers," Charity said in a tone of disbelief. "My own lieutenant. The guy who recruited me. He let me take the fall."

Travis nodded. "You were the perfect scapegoat. Fresh. Vulnerable. Easy to discredit."

Charity whispered, "We were friends."

"He was everyone's friend," Travis replied. "Smart. Funny. The chief's golden child."

Charity shook her head. The news fell like a chandelier that had its chain cut. She hadn't realized how much guilt she'd still been carrying—how some part of her still wondered if she *had* made a mistake… or if she somehow deserved what happened.

"I thought I was going crazy," she said. "The gaslighting. The silence. Being treated like I was a criminal."

"You're not crazy," Travis said. "You saw the rot before anyone else. You were a threat. That's why they had to get rid of you."

Charity and Travis continued talking late into the night—former coworkers and one-time enemies who saw their lives in a different light.

44

The key stuck a little in the lock, as it always did when the sun was high. Charity jiggled it once, then twice, before the deadbolt clicked free. She pushed the door open and stepped into the apartment. It wasn't much—just two rooms, a galley kitchen, and a creaky old fan. But it was hers.

She set her bag down on the thrift store end table and slipped off her shoes by the door, her toes pressing into the cool laminate floor. The light filtered through gauzy curtains she'd picked up at the secondhand store, turning the walls a soft, forgiving gold.

There were still boxes in the corner. A few clothes hung in the closet. But it felt like a beginning.

She walked to the small desk in the corner and pulled open the drawer. Inside was a checkbook ledger, a bank statement, and a handwritten note that read:

Pay yourself first. Always.

She smiled, tracing the edge of the deposit receipt with her fingertip. Her new account wasn't large, but it was growing.

Every tip. Every shift. She was building a savings account.

She crossed the room to the hall closet and opened the door to put away a pillow and blanket.

There, neatly stacked on the bottom shelf, was a folded blue tarp, a rolled-up tent, and a weather-stained backpack, its zipper still frayed where she'd tried to fix it with a paperclip. She crouched down and brushed her hand across the fabric.

Memories swelled—mornings beside the fire, rain-soaked nights, the cold ache of shame, the silence between the old world and whatever came next.

A tear slipped down her cheek.

She stood and wiped it away.

Out back, the air smelled of earth and sun.

A narrow strip of lawn bordered the wooden fence, and in the corner, beneath the shade of a crooked fir tree, was her garden.

A real one.

Dirt and mulch and compost.

She had dug it with her own hands.

Tomato sprouts peeked from the dark soil.

Marigolds ringed the edge like golden sentries.

A single cucumber vine had started to stretch its way up the makeshift trellis she had built.

She knelt in the soil and pressed her fingers into the dirt.

The ground gave way.

Not like it used to—dry and reluctant—but soft.

Ready.

She smiled.

She wasn't surviving.

She was thriving.

EPILOGUE

The scent of cinnamon and espresso drifted through the air, mingling with the warm hum of conversation and the low hiss of steamed milk.

Charity moved through the café with practiced grace, a cloth in one hand, a coffee order in the other. The bell above the front door chimed softly behind her. Someone had just entered, but she didn't turn to look.

Sunlight poured through the wide front windows, casting honeyed streaks across the polished concrete floor. It was different here—less gray, less damp, less heavy than the world she had left behind.

The walls were the color of sand and morning light.

The pace was slower.

The warmth was real.

She stopped mid-stride, drawn by the flicker of a bird outside.

A cactus stood tall beside the building's edge, its green limbs reaching toward the sky like a strange, holy sculpture.

A desert breeze stirred the wind chimes overhead.

She turned her attention back to the table by the window.

"Two lattes," she said with a smile, setting them down. "One sweet, one bold."

The couple thanked her. Their voices faded into the background as she made her way to the back, through a rustic swinging door that led to a narrow hallway and a small office tucked in the rear corner of the shop.

She sat at the desk, pulling the schedule from the bulletin board. Notes were scribbled in the margins—*Tina can't work Thursdays. Tom wants more weekend hours.* It wasn't overwhelming. It felt… alive.

This place wasn't just a job. It was hers.

She opened her laptop and scrolled through a vendor order. Syrups. Cups. Beans from a new roaster in Tucson. She caught her reflection in the screen—lighter. Older. But content in a way she had never felt before.

A knock came from the side door. She looked up.

A woman stood in the doorway.

Dark hair.

Her arms crossed tight, not for warmth, but for defense.

Faint scars lined the inside of her forearms—slender reminders of a past lived on the edge. Her eyes were wide and uncertain.

"Hi," the woman said softly. "I saw the sign in the window… about the job."

Charity didn't answer right away. She took in the posture, the pain behind the voice. The trembling hope barely holding shape.

She smiled. "What's your name?"

"Shiloh Martinez."

Charity gestured to the chair across from her. "Come in, Shiloh," she said. "Have a seat."

ABOUT THE AUTHOR

Praying Medic (Dave Hayes) is an author, retired paramedic, and podcaster. He's written hundreds of articles and dozens of books—both fiction and non-fiction. He writes about the miracles God has done through his ministry with the goal of teaching others to live as ambassadors of God's kingdom. His books, articles, and videos inspire and challenge believers to enter into a deeper relationship with God. Dave is a licensed amateur radio operator. During his 35-year career as a paramedic, he taught advanced cardiac and basic trauma life support, high-angle rescue, and community preparedness.

Other books from Praying Medic
For up-to-date titles go to: PrayingMedic.com

The first novel in the series you just read:
The Gates of Shiloh

Series—The Kingdom of God Made Simple:
Divine Healing Made Simple
Seeing in the Spirit Made Simple
Hearing God's Voice Made Simple
Traveling in the Spirit Made Simple
Dream Interpretation Made Simple
Power and Authority Made Simple
Emotional Healing Made Simple

Series—The Courts of Heaven:
Defeating Your Adversary in the Court of Heaven
Operating in the Court of Angels

Series—My Craziest Adventures with God:
My Craziest Adventures with God - Volume 1
My Craziest Adventures with God - Volume 2

And more:
Emotional Healing in 3 Easy Steps
Emergency Preparedness and Off-Grid Communication
God Speaks: Perspectives on Hearing God's Voice (28 authors)
A Kingdom View of Economic Collapse (eBook only)
American Sniper: Lessons in Spiritual Warfare (eBook only)

SCAN THIS TO GO TO
PrayingMedic.com

www.ingramcontent.com/pod-product-compliance
Lightning Source LLC
Chambersburg PA
CBHW030520080526
44586CB00011B/269